Fierce Consciousness:

Surviving the Sorrows
of Earth and Self

For Ed –
In gratitude,
Trebbe Johnson

Also by Trebbe Johnson

You've Made the Earth More Beautiful!

Radical Joy for Hard Times: Finding Meaning and Making Beauty in Earth's Broken Places

101 Ways to Make Guerrilla Beauty

The World Is a Waiting Lover: Desire and the Quest for the Beloved

Fierce Consciousness:

Surviving the Sorrows
of Earth and Self

Trebbe Johnson

Calliope Books

Ithaca, New York

Fierce Consciousness: Surviving the Sorrows of Earth and Self

ISBN: 979-8-218-06389-4

Printed in the United States of America
First Printing, 2023

Book design by Cris Wanzer

For

Eli Gardner
Gideon Hewitt
Isaiah Gardner
Augustus (Gus) Greenberg

May you find and make beauty every day.

... bright power, dark peace;
Fierce consciousness joined with final
Disinterestedness;
Life with calm death; the falcon's
Realist eyes and act
Married to the massive
Mysticism of stone...

Robinson Jeffers, from "Rock and Hawk"

CONTENTS

❋

❋

PROLOGUE

You are Sisyphus. Now What?

You are Sisyphus, and so am I. You're worried sick, tired out, scared for the world and scared for your own small part of the world, which is the only part you have any control over, except sometimes you feel you have absolutely no control over anything. You are heaving an enormous boulder up a mountain with no guarantee that it's going to stay put, even if you manage to settle it up there at the summit. Truth be told, there are times when you think there might not even be a summit, that life will be nothing but an endless march through despair from this point on. Yet what can you do? You keep going. You push. You push because your life depends on it.

In Greek myth, Sisyphus was a whistleblower. He informed a man that he'd seen the king of the gods, unmistakable even though he was at that moment disguised as an eagle, in the act of abducting the man's daughter. Zeus learned about Sisyphus' indiscretion and punished that mortal man by exiling him to the Underworld, where he had to roll a rock up a mountain, only to watch it tumble back down to the bottom as soon as he'd settled it on the peak. This was to be his single task for all eternity. There was no escaping it, no work-arounds, no hope, no possible rescue from a more sympathetic Olympian deity.

You are Sisyphus. You live in a world scourged by a lethal virus, the rise of extreme nationalism and racism, and a planetary ecosystem that can no longer support its billion beautiful species, including your own human species, the way it used to do. As if that weren't so unreasonably hard a task to manage, you're also bearing your own personal griefs, whether that means joblessness, a scary medical diagnosis, unhappy kids, rejection, addiction, debt, abuse in the home or on the job. The list is endless, and it shifts in ways you can't anticipate and can't adequately respond to. Now what? How will you get through this? How will any of us get through all this? And yet, like Sisyphus, we do. As Albert Camus wrote at the end of his essay about the myth, "one must imagine Sisyphus happy," for at every moment of his existence he confronts his rocklike reality and throws his whole weight behind it.

The United States was in the sixth month of the coronavirus pandemic when my husband died. Andy had had bladder cancer for about seven years, but as far as his doctor had assured us just three months before, it was manageable, non-invasive, and non-aggressive. In July his health started to decline. He lost his appetite and tired easily. On August 4 I took him to the hospital emergency room. For three days the doctors hid their knowledge behind their professional gazes, reporting that they needed the pathology report before they could tell us anything. Finally, a palliative care doctor let us know that the cancer had spread to his liver and stomach and he didn't have much time left. Andy died in a hospice facility five days later.

So. The worst thing in my life had happened, the thing I had been dreading. The thing I had tried to prepare myself for ever since I fell in love with that creative, sexy, sweet and brilliant man. I was alone. An hour after he died, after I had called his three grown children and a few friends and packed up all our things, I walked out of the hospice building on a hot summer's midnight to be greeted by katydids singing in the trees all around me. The beauty of their voices shot right into me. I put down my bags and just listened in amazement. That song plucked me up for one full moment and then dropped me hard back down on the pavement, bruised with gratitude. Beauty and sorrow, joy and ugliness co-exist. I had known it since I was a little girl and now, at the worst time of my life, that truth grabbed and shook me again. Many people assume that sorrow and beauty are enemies, but they aren't. In fact, you could say they're lovers. They exhibit their own radiance most fully when their partner is on stage. When you make friends with one, you get its wild soulmate as well.

In the midst of suffering, it is possible to be seized by inexplicable joy. The feeling is different from happiness, which lilts you along and makes you feel content. Joy doesn't have a lot of staying power, but it has amazing loft. So startling is this joy, so apparently out of place that its sudden arrival can seem like sacrilege. *How could it be possible for me to radiate under such circumstances?* demands your inner moralist. *Surely something is wrong with you. Have you, in fact, lost your mind?* Perhaps your reaction is to tamp down such an apparently unreasonable elation, deeming it utterly inappropriate, perhaps even immoral. It is true that such joy is "radical." It is outrageous, startling, ridiculous. It has no precedent. It is illogical. It is a life-saver.

We all have ways of coping with grief and loss. Sometimes we react by finding someone or something to blame and then devoting ourselves to anger or revenge. At times our inclination is to stay busy, shove our sorrow into a closet and tell ourselves and others that we're coping just fine. Or we become helpless, incapable of acting on our own behalf and demanding that someone else, please, anyone, pick up the pieces of our lives. Or we tell ourselves we don't have to worry, that everything will be all right in the end, because God or science or Gaia herself will take care of the problem. There is another way. It is possible to find and even generate joy and meaning and a sense of purpose in the midst of sorrow. No matter what has knocked us down or how long we've been there, we can not only survive but thrive. Flattened by grief, we can yet be pierced by beauty, wonder, and delight. These gifts come unpredictably, on their own time table, not necessarily when we think we need them. They transcend categories. They are sneaky and whimsical like elves. They arrive in the form of an act of kindness from a stranger at the gas pump or the scent of a rose on the worst day of your life. Such darts of beauty are as abrupt and undeviating as raptor birds. They swoop down, sweep you up, spirit you away. Yes, they'll drop you down again, and you'll know the problem you've been facing hasn't changed. But you'll be different. You'll know that life plows on and soars on, even though you seem to be stuck. You'll know that, even in the depths of your sorrow, you can be reached by the extraordinary, and that, if you pay attention, you will surely be plucked up again. As poets and sages throughout the ages, from Rumi to Leonard Cohen, have reminded us, it's only when a vessel is cracked that the light gets through.

Discovering how to exist alongside beauty means not only seeing or hearing it, but also becoming possessed of a new impulse to give it away. This inclination, this outward manifestation of the innermost self doesn't happen all at once. It moves, in fact, in a way that's just the opposite of beauty's fleet, unerring arrow. An impulse to reach beyond yourself to gently touch some aspect of the world may feel at first like an odd little impulse you're tempted to brush away. Walk past the campaign sign touting the candidate you can't stand in order to bring flowers to a neighbor whose partner has just died? Let a friend or colleague know about some trait of theirs that you really admire? Pause as you stride down a city sidewalk to touch the trunk of a slender, flowering tree? A little tug within you urges, *Go on!* But another, repellant force frets: *What would people think? Maybe some other time, not now.* Yet saying Yes to that little tug usually calls forth not frowns or snide laughter, but absolute indifference on the part of witnesses, pleasure from the recipient, and an emboldening boost of joy for you, the giver.

I have experienced the deaths of several loved ones, dangerous alcoholism in my family and in myself, and a personal variation on the kinds of disappointments we all suffer because we happen to have been born as human beings with dreams. For decades I've been grieving the demise of nature and the declining health of Planet Earth and practicing something I call "radical joy" to find and create beauty in broken places.. Throughout the worst of times, I have been periodically seized by bursts of awe and astonishment. I wrote this book to share what I've learned about surviving—and even transforming—grief and loss, a process that requires a kind of fierce consciousness. Fierce consciousness is the expectation—unfailingly met—that extraordinary beauty will burst into dark places at any moment, but that to receive it, one has to keep the antennae of perception wide open. The teachers who passed their wisdom on to me were not the kind at whose feet you sit for years, trying to absorb their wisdom and feeling stupid for not getting it. My teachers imparted their lessons quickly, sometimes in just a few seconds and often without words. They were katydids, a glimpse of ocean, a stranger in a subway, a line from a TV show, and grief itself. Without fierce consciousness I would have missed their profound teachings.

How can we can live with the death of the Earth, especially knowing that we have caused it? What water can we eat or drink that is pure, not laced with chemicals or clotted with invisible pieces of plastic? How can we educate and comfort our children and grandchildren, that they can help themselves and others live with what a world of greed and acquisitiveness and the refusal to say "enough" have wrought? What festivals or practices of atonement, of gratitude, of consolation, shall we have to invent? How can we care for the places we love and care for ourselves in the process, when those places have been leveled by fire, flood, or extreme wind? How can we be open, always, to the song of katydids?

The dire problems facing every one of us planetary citizens in the twenty-first century demand a new kind of heroism. We need to dedicate ourselves to authenticity, courage, and compassion as we face these great challenges, personal and global. We need to claim different kinds of superpowers. No longer can we be lone rangers galloping away from our bold deeds into remote hideaways. No longer can we define the existence of others by what they wear or the color of their skin or what we assume about their gender or know about their politics. No longer can we assume that only humans are entitled to thrive to their fullest extent. We need to be braver and we need to pay more attention to the allurements of the world. We need to nourish our inner lives and embolden our outer lives. And we need all the tools we can get.

This book contains some simple tools for how to live, not just through the hard times themselves, but any day. It offers actions and ways to think about those actions that give them meaning and relevance. The five sections—*Sink, Punch, Seek, Receive,* and *Give*— plot a path for dealing with challenge. It begins with acknowledging a bad situation (*Sink*), but refusing to be overrun by it (*Punch*). *Seek* offers suggestions for opening up to inspiration and even delight when you're stuck in the muck of life and feel like there's no way out. *Receive* explores some of the many simple opportunities for opening up to wonder, even in the throes of enormous grief and turmoil. *Give* shows the power of reaching outward in spontaneous, seemingly minor ways that can change the trajectory of a whole day. After you've read the book all the way through, you can open it at random now and then, read a chapter, and see where it leads you.

Fierce consciousness is about braiding attitude, actions, and attention together into a single strong and colorful strand. It's about co-existing with ourselves, others, and the world around us in a way that becomes part of life, into and through the hard times, and that can inspire us, inform us, and make us bigger people, capable of actions we never thought possible—and often weren't possible until we ourselves enacted them. It's about facing the doubt and chaos and fear of what we're living through without tearing each other apart or falling into such gloom that we want to give up. Finally, it's about how, even in the most unlikely of circumstances, it is possible to live through hard times with integrity, while giving and receiving abundant beauty, meaning, and joy.

I. SINK

There's no getting around it. Grief will not be ignored or bargained with. The only way to live with grief is to drop down into its dark, dank, grimy lair and wrestle with it. And by wrestling I don't mean trying to shove it to the back of your mind or reason with it or whip yourself into asserting that things could be worse. I mean being willing to face the bleakness, the hopelessness, the utter agony of the thing. I mean kicking and screaming and getting pummeled by grief. In the intimate company of grief you wail. You feel like one more sob will yank the guts right out of your belly. It hurts, sometimes excruciatingly. But when you meet grief head-on, it usually overwhelms you only for a finite time. When you avoid grief, it lingers interminably. And eventually, you are released. The confrontation may need to happen again—in fact it probably will—but each time you will be released.

1. Refuse to disbelieve.

Yes, I thought. I put the book down on the study hall table and stared out the window at the winter trees in the school's back yard. *Yes. I understand this. I, too, know what it is to disbelieve and why it is the one thing I absolutely must not do.*

Albert Camus's novel *La Peste (The Plague)* opens as a lethal rat-borne disease begins to overtake a North African city. At first, most of the citizens refuse to admit that they are under threat. They assure themselves that the illness is nothing much to worry about and will soon pass. They "disbelieved in the plague," Camus writes. "They thought that everything still was possible for them; which presupposed that pestilences were impossible. They went on doing business, arranged for journeys, and formed views. How should they have given a thought to anything like plague, which rules out any future, cancels journeys, silences the exchange of views." [1] Eventually, as they watch their neighbors being carried out of their homes on stretchers, and as they peer down at their own fathers or wives or children, covered with boils and shaking with fever in their beds, they can no longer deny the truth. The government officials formally declare an epidemic and order the city gates locked. No one can get in or out. The plague settles—irrevocable, unyielding, indiscriminate. Along with plans and journeys, hope, too, gradually fades and, says Camus, "nothing was left us but a series of present moments."

We were reading the novel in my advanced high school French class. At seventeen, I was sure that Camus had had someone just like me in mind as his ideal reader. I looked down at my Livre de Poche edition, with its cover of a spectral human figure staring down a hillside as rats race toward a stylized Middle Eastern city on the sea. *Yes*, I thought again, *I know disbelief.* I'd seen it in my own family, repeatedly. When my father got drunk, he got mean. He would find things to accuse my mother of and then, when he had fueled his sense of injustice with more gin, he started hitting her. By the age of eight I had trained myself to lie awake in bed, breath-bated and board-stiff, waiting for the shift in sounds—the gradual slurring of his words, the sudden rise in the volume of his reproach, a slap, her voice pleading, a smack, a thump, her cry, a thud. Then it was time to get out of bed and run downstairs to plead with him. When I couldn't pull him away from her, I would run to the kitchen phone and call the police, who, when they arrived, were easily jollied by my father into accepting that his daughter was a little high-strung and this was simply a disagreement between husband and wife. Sometimes my mother and my little brother and I would flee across the lawn and knock on the door of one of our neighbors, who would obligingly turn down the sheets for us in a guest room or make up a bed on the sun porch. In the morning, the dew soaked the cuffs of our pajamas as we walked back across the lawn to our house. My father was waiting for us, hunched over a cup of coffee at the dining room table. He was full of contrition. He promised he would never act like that again, and we had to go to him and be gathered into his arms and hugged. His skin was hot and smelled of decomposing wood. My mother always seemed to believe him and so, to protect her, I pretended that I believed too. But I had realized that things were not going to get better and might get worse. I figured there was a likelihood that, one of these nights, my father was going to kill my mother. My brother was too young to grasp this truth. My mother was apparently unwilling to do so. She disbelieved in the plague in our home. Clearly, therefore, it was my responsibility, and mine alone, to grab hold of the truth. If I was prepared, I thought, I would not get sucked into a falsity that could destroy us all. I kept my knowledge to myself and felt old and sad and burdened by it. But I would not disbelieve.

Years after I first read *The Plague*, the concept of stubborn disbelief in the face of undeniable reality struck me as an apt metaphor for the attitude so many people had, or claimed to have, about climate change. Proudly scoffing at the irrefutable evidence of science, some politicians and the spokespeople of petrochemical companies calmly, and seemingly rationally, claimed that all the facts about Earth's future added up to nothing so much as a hoax or, at best, a big exaggeration. If it was cold outside, then the planet wasn't warming! If the seas were rising, well, they'd risen before. A million years ago. So what was wrong with that? You could look at it positively. Maybe there would be orange groves in Vermont, for example. The motive of some of these self-proclaimed disbelievers was plain: admitting a problem would necessitate fixing it, and fixing it would be expensive. If a corporation perceived a problem with the way they were doing business, they might make a few discreet adjustments, but to make the need for any such adjustments public would damage credibility and cost a lot of money. Exxon, for example, denied the reality of climate change for decades, even as they rebuilt their oil rig platforms higher in the Gulf of Mexico, so they would not be inundated by rising waters caused by rapidly melting ice in the poles. As Bill McKibben told this story at the 2015 Bioneers Conference in San Rafael, California and elaborated on it in his book *Falter*, published four years later: "So: global warming is the ultimate problem of oil companies because oil causes it, and it's the ultimate problem for government haters because without government intervention, you can't solve it. Those twin existential threats, to cash and to worldview, meant that there was never any shortage of resources for the task of denying climate change."[2]

The predictions, the graphs, the apocalyptic movies, the lectures, the melting, the emaciated polar bears, the empty black window screen in mid-summer where insects used to flutter and grapple— the manifestations of climate change clump together into a reality it's hard to bear. If you are a sensible, right-thinking human, you despair, because there is no stopping this thing, not now, not after half a century of warnings ignored and an ongoing determination to disbelieve. As Extinction Rebellion has often declared, "THIS IS AN EMERGENCY." Yes, and even as we acknowledge this emergency, we still want to look the other way. As the meteorologist

Adam Sobel has noted, humans are intrinsically incapable of preparing for extravagantly rare events. And what could be more rare than the end of the world?

Then, in the early weeks of 2020, the world was hit with a real-life plague. Unlike erratic and impersonal forces of destruction such as wildfire, hurricane, and flooding, the coronavirus snatched its victims individually and personally. As the disease swept through Wuhan, China and health officials in Europe warned that it was on the move and highly infectious, it was easy for us in what we thought was the far-off safety zone of the United States to feel immune. Even as the American death rate climbed to more than two thousand a day for several days in a row, and hospitals ran out of beds for sick people, there were those who still disbelieved. Some churches continued to hold Sunday services. College students flirted, drank beer, and tanned on Florida beaches during spring break. There were people who claimed it was all a hoax. As the November presidential election approached, supporters of Donald Trump gathered, unmasked, at political rallies. The president himself got sick, and still he claimed that the United States had "turned the corner" on the virus. As the disease spiked once again that autumn, many dying patients in the hardest hit states of South Dakota, Iowa, and Wisconsin raged at their nurses, who, they insisted, were lying about the diagnosis. "Their last dying words are, 'This can't be happening. It's not real,'" a South Dakota emergency room nurse, Jodi Doering, said, adding that some patients were adamant they were dying from pneumonia or lung cancer, not COVID-19.

It's normal to react to bad news by heading right away for the flimsy but seductive door that promises to get you the hell out of there and into a safer interpretation of what you're up against. Disbelief, or denial, is the first step in the pattern Elisabeth Kübler-Ross defined as constituting the five stages of grief. If your doctor gently informs you that you have a terminal disease, your whole being might scream *NO!* You are innocent and have done absolutely nothing to deserve this blow. You've never been trained for such a thing and can't possibly take the time to begin learning now. Of course you want to deny this reality! *No!* It happens even when the calamity is sky-high, incandescent, and right in front of you. In 2014 the French photographer Bernard Hermann had published a book, *Paris km 00*, with photographs of Notre Dame taken from his apartment window. When he saw the cathedral in flames in April 2019, he couldn't face it. "I was thunderstruck," he said. "I closed the curtains." Of course he did not *disbelieve* that this beloved Parisian icon was on fire; he simply could not, at that moment, face such a terrible reality.

The two terms, *disbelief* and *denial*, are close in meaning, but denial is actually refutation of something real, whereas disbelief is more of a conviction that the fact itself is not true. Disbelief turns its back on a bad reality; denial keeps on facing it but makes fun of it or tweaks it so it doesn't look so bad. Neither disbelief nor denial is always a bad thing. There are times when we need them to survive, to make informed decisions about the choices before us. If you answer the phone and the person on the other end informs you that this is the IRS calling and there's a problem with your taxes, and all they need is your social security number to fix it, there's no better response than vehement disbelief and a quick move to end the call.

It's actually easy to disbelieve in climate change because, unlike the calamities for which it is responsible, like tornados or droughts, climate change is not a thing with a form you can point to and say, "There it is—climate change!" Environmental philosopher Timothy Morton calls climate change a *hyperobject*, a phenomenon that powerfully exists, even though you can't see it, touch it, aim your weapons at it, or coax it to settle down. Hyperobjects, says Morton, are "viscous, which means that they 'stick' to beings that are involved with them. They are nonlocal; in other words, any 'local manifestation' of a hyperobject is not directly the hyperobject."[3] Snowstorms in Atlanta are evidence of climate change, but they are not climate change itself.

Refusing to disbelieve doesn't necessarily mean that I will

6

immediately know how to respond to whatever emergency confronts me. It simply means I am planting my feet on the firm ground of where I am. If I can't get past disbelief, I will wobble, stumble, vacillate, and often make bad decisions. The situation itself will buffet me, even as I keep on telling myself that buffeting cannot possibly befall me. My mother accepted my father's promises of "never again" for years. It wasn't until I was eleven and he told her that he was having an affair that she finally filed for divorce. She had been willing to live with physical abuse, but could not sanction infidelity. Yet she took the step she had to take to free herself from all of it. The temptation "to hole up in the refuge of one's own psyche," wrote Hannah Arendt of the willingness of millions of Germans to fall under the sway of the Nazis, will always result in "a loss of humanness along with the forsaking of reality."[4] The psyche, left alone, is not a safe place to be when a bad reality needs dealing with.

Some realities are more easily confronted than others. I can fix a leaky faucet, change the cartridges in the printer, or call the dentist when I have a toothache, but I can't reverse climate change, outrun a pandemic, or heal a loved one who's sick. I saw my husband's life sweep right out of his body at the moment he died, and there wasn't a cell in my being that didn't know he was gone. Yet often in the anguish of the months that followed, I found myself crying out to him, "Come back, come back! Please don't leave me!" It was not the rational, competent part of me that wailed so desperately, it was an instinctive rejection of mental and emotional pain. That abject, wailing soul, curled in a fetal position on the rug, was the stubborn, atavistic disbeliever in me. You've probably got one too—a figment of your self that digs in its heels and refuses to believe a certain truth. I'd warrant that even Bill McKibben's got one somewhere in his courageous, indefatigable, bellwether soul. In those moments we are not denying. We know the thing is real and ugly and dire. But we just want to turn our backs for a moment. We just need a little break. I find my own inner disbeliever kicking in when I read some horrifying new article about the rapid melting of glaciers or the number of fatalities from yet another school shooting in the United States, and I just can't deal with it right then. I turn my back on it. I don't exactly disbelieve, but that part of me that wants to do exactly that is vehemently insisting, "Don't trouble yourself with this! Do something else! Now!" After a break, that inner rebel calms down. For those who insist climate change or the presidency of Joe Biden or Covid isn't real, the rebel has taken over.

Eventually, I must be willing to face my reality and be slugged by it. I must agree to accept this new state of things and start getting familiar with it. Yes, I may crumble. Yes, panic or grief may sear my entire body, and I will doubt that I can ever recover. And yet, I recover. It doesn't happen until I make room for reality. No recovery is possible until I admit I have a problem. No healing is possible until I admit I have a disease. No reconciliation is possible until I admit there's been a breach in the relationship. I refuse to disbelieve.

2. Drop into the well of grief.

Once we refuse to live in denial or disbelief, we are able to drop into what poet David Whyte calls "the well of grief." Refusing to disbelieve is the decision to go ahead and confront a bad situation. What happens next is that the situation takes its turn in the partnership and reaches out to interact with us. Often what it pulls forth is our grief. Unless we let ourselves fall into that well, we won't be able to climb out of it.

What now?

You hesitate. Fear of the destructive power of the grief you've kept at bay flays your very being. You tell yourself you've been managing okay. Yes, sorrow gnaws at you like a dog attacking a chew-toy. Is grief really necessary? you ask yourself. Haven't you begun to live with this absence that has attacked your life—the loss of your lover, your forest, your career, your cat, your wedding ring? Yes, the hole of what was there follows you around and reminds you of the presence it once contained, but you are waking up every day, eating and peeing, standing and sitting, and still able to form words. So you are doing all right, aren't you? You're managing the grief.

Yet there comes a day when you know there is still something that must be done. You must descend into the well. Your gut imagines the dark and bumpy drop to the bottom, the likelihood of never escaping. And yet, it is this very thing you fear that you finally allow yourself to do, for you know that, if you don't, you will never experience either the real anguish or the stubborn resilience of your own self rebounding from it.

And so you drop. The black bite of it grabs hold of you, and you drop and drop and drop. When it seems you can drop no more, you keep dropping. The well of grief is deep, and in those moments when you are dropping, you feel your life can't last much longer. Perhaps you will survive, you will keep on breathing, but no light will ever shine for or from you again. And then, almost always

9

sooner than you have expected, something happens. For me it's as if the well of grief, having received me, wants nothing more to do with me. For a woman I know whose son took his own life, it's as if an angel is waiting down there at the bottom to catch her before she shatters. Either way, you discover that the bottom of the well is not a dank, stinking floor, but a trampoline, and it's bouncing you out.

And so you have done it. You have dropped down into the well of grief, and you have returned. The grief has become part of you now. It is streaming through your blood, no longer blocked in one stiff, untouchable place. Grief has become part of your authentic being. As the saxophonist and composer Branford Marsalis once said about the blues, the fact that you recognize that you are sad is a very freeing and liberating experience.[1]

Probably it is not over. Grief will want you back again. Someone told me after Andy died that grief is love with nowhere to go. The one you loved is gone, but the love itself bubbles and churns and wants to be given, and there is no one to give it to. So you must drop into the well again, and it will hurt again. Maybe this time the drop will not be so steep and the imprisonment within it will not be so long. Maybe you will get bounced up a little sooner. But now you know that you can enter the well of grief and, as Whyte says, experience "the source from which we drink." In his *Wild Edge of Sorrow* Francis Weller, who has written and taught widely on the subject of grief, points out that, "While it is difficult to embrace grief and be moved by its muscular demands, without it we would not know the heartening quality of compassion, could not experience the full breadth of love, the surprise of joy, we could not celebrate the sheer beauty of the world. Grief fosters each of these capabilities, deepening them by bringing gravity to the moment."[2]

Love leads to sorrow, and sorrow leads to love. Chris Jordan is an American photographer who takes pictures of the innards of baby albatrosses who have died because their parents unwittingly fed them krill and squid clogged with plastic waste, and the digestive system of the little birds can't handle it. Jordan made a film about the birds, because he is forthright about his love for them, and he wants others to love them too. "I want people to watch this film and feel sadness and rage and realize that comes from a place of love," he said. "Don't pull the plug out of the bathtub just yet; don't let all that raw emotion drain away. Once you feel love, you can be more courageous and make more radical choices." Unless we open up to our sorrow, we will never fall in love with the miracle of life prevailing in the midst of grief or discover rare and lovely treasures half-buried in the grit of our darkest emotions.

After Andy died, I had to topple into that terrible well of grief every day, often several times a day. Sometimes grief engulfed me before I could prepare myself, as it did one day when I was driving home and passed the farm where a resident donkey grazed the green pasture among a herd of Holsteins. Andy was enchanted by that donkey. He would look for it when we drove by, and if he didn't see it, would comment. Sometimes he'd say in way that might have been serious, but that he took care to express with some levity, "Maybe we should get a donkey." There, now, was the donkey, yet there was no Andy to see her. I had to pull over and stop the car. The donkey and the cows were close enough that they would have heard my wails. And then, after a few minutes, I floated back up, blew my nose, and drove on.

Many indigenous cultures regard ceremonies of grief and healing as essential practices that keep the community healthy. A medicine man or woman of the Haudenosaunee nations in the area that is now New York State and southern Quebec offer a Condolence Ceremony after someone has died, inviting mourners to dry their eyes, open their ears, and make new footprints as they step back into their life. Among the Lakota, saying goodbye includes an evening gathering when family and friends get together to swap stories about the deceased and choose for themselves an object that had belonged to him or her. For Balinese Hindus saying goodbye to a loved one is a complex community ceremony meant to assure that the soul of the deceased is welcomed into its place with the gods, from whence it will eventually reincarnate into another member of the family. The men of the village craft an elaborate sarcophagus in the shape of an animal in which to place the body and a cremation tower, or *bade*, representing the entire universe, in which they lay the sarcophagus. Meanwhile, the women of the village are making many different kinds of offerings of flowers, rice, and other treats for the gods. The family members of the deceased must keep everyone who's working on these preparations fed and supplied with cigarettes. On the day of the cremation, chosen because a priest has deemed it auspicious, members of the village carry the *bade* through the village to the cemetery, frequently pausing to turn it round and round as they shout and holler, precautions to confuse the spirit and prevent it from wandering back to its former home and disturbing the family. After the body is burned, there is another procession, this time to the sea, to which the ashes are given in a final ceremony of purification. When a Balinese person dies, loved ones are expected to weep for ten days only. After that, indulging in tears is thought to be a selfish act that will hold the dead person back from the next life that awaits them. Guiding all these traditional practices is a commitment to a future in which both the individual who has died and those who survive must continue to prosper.

In Weller's workshops, participants create a shrine with photos of loved ones who have died, animal and plant species that have become extinct, and places that have been destroyed. They make this shrine over a couple of days, and then it is time for the grief ceremony. As soon as the invocation for it is complete, some people rush to the shrine, sink to the floor, and begin wailing. Their grief overflows and can be contained no longer. For others the process is slower, quieter, but no less impactful. No one is alone at the altar of grief. Each person is attended by one other whose responsibility is to be present only for them, to touch a quivering shoulder, to offer a lap to cry on, or simply to be a witness.

The message is clear: the soundest and safest way to recover from grief is to grieve with trusted others, so that a build-up of unexpressed sorrow doesn't shred the fabric of the community. In *The Wild Edge of Sorrow* Weller relates a story about an Italian-American community in Roseto, Pennsylvania. Because people there had a very low incidence of heart disease, they sparked a lot of interest among health care researchers in the 1960s. The researchers could find no obvious reason for the longevity of their subjects. Many of the men worked in slate quarries, where they were susceptible to lung diseases. People smoked, didn't get a lot of exercise, and ate high-fat diets. The researchers concluded that it was the closeness of the multigenerational families that was responsible for the community's good health. Sadly, it all began to change in the following decade as more of Roseto's young people went to college and then stayed away, the oldest family members died, and adults moved out of homes where several generations had lived together and settled in single-family houses. Heart-disease rates began to rise. "It wasn't good habits or diet that had been protecting people's hearts for all those decades," Weller writes. "It was connection."

Here is a well of grief we're going to have to drop into over and over again for all our lives, no matter if we are eighty or eight: the wrecking power of climate change. In the years, the generations to come, we're going to have to cry more than once for the losses this awful human-caused streak of change will wreak. We will cry for the homes we love and lose. We will cry for the ever diminishing numbers and variety of warblers who sing in our woodlands each year. We will cry because our governments, which were supposed to protect its citizens, cared only about protecting their economic interests and did so little to accommodate the looming crisis. We will cry for the rivers and lakes that are drying up and for the schools and churches that are rotting in rainwater. We will cry for all the people who have no place to go. We will cry for all we took for granted, including summer vacations at the other end of a plane and the accessibility of heat on a winter day and cool on a summer day and the easy availability of toys and makeup and sweaters made all over the world and delivered to our doorstep in just days. The sorrow will be deep and it will be recurrent.

"Time in its passage does not carry away with it these impossible projects," wrote the French philosopher Marcel Merleau-Ponty. The "projects" he refers to are the ways in which we must traverse the long roads of life in sorrow. We continue to be, in some sense, the person we were when we loved and relied on that person or thing which we know will never return to us.[3] We heal from the wound, yet the wounding itself and our own suffering on account of it remain embedded in our life, our psyche, our own unique presence in the world. This is the scar our drop into the well etches on us. Grief of any kind torques and tortures us until, finally, we are able to start recreating a life in and around the spaces of what is missing. And even then the scar remains. The scar is a sign of love.

3. Stop making sense.

Whenever there's a disaster, human-made or natural, journalists can't help reporting that the people in the affected community "are trying to make sense" of what happened.

"We're all trying to do the right things. We're all trying to make sense of this," says a reporter on a Madison, Wisconsin TV broadcast about the coronavirus. A *New York Times* article about a tornado that whipped through Monson, Massachusetts begins, "Stunned residents of this small, tightly knit town spent Thursday trying to make sense of something most of them thought just did not happen here: a powerful, tornado that tore houses off their foundations, ripped off roofs, sheared the tops of some trees and tossed power lines around like string." Commenting on the massacre of fifty-nine people by a man who checked into a Las Vegas hotel room with several suitcases full of automatic rifles that he methodically fired down on concert goers, an expert in post-traumatic stress disorder stated, "Our minds don't rest easily not knowing the cause of something so baffling and monstrous and shocking. We'd like to be able to organize that experience, to put a box around it, with arrows to say, 'OK, x led to y.'" Are the people who have undergone these calamities really seeking some reason why they occurred, or are these comments merely forms of a catchphrase journalists have come to inject into their stories as a way of acknowledging that physical events have emotional consequences? Either way, the statement implies that, if only we humans were privy to the roots of a new and terrible mystery, we might be able to cope better with it.

In many cases, it is possible to piece together a logical progression of causes for an event. Take climate change, for example. It's happening because excessive amounts of carbon dioxide, emitted by the systems that power the world through the heating of fossil fuels and by the burning of rain forests, creates a barrier in the atmosphere that traps the emissions of those fuels instead of radiating them back into space. The result is an overheated planet. It is also possible to account for the atmospheric origins of the tornado that ravaged Monson. As for the mass murder of all those innocent concert goers, the FBI announced after investigating the case for a year that they could find "no single or clear motivating factor" for the action.

But, really, when you're trying to muddle through tragedy, what you want most is to get through this! You want things to be better. You want to quit worrying all the time. You want to get through just one day without bursting into tears or feeling your body ice up with dread. My husband might have disagreed. On the day he entered the hospice facility Andy informed a team of doctors that he could not die until they had the pathology report back from the lab and he knew what he was dying from. I had to laugh. The doctors shot startled eyes at me. "It's so like him," I told them, "always curious about the way things work." I thought about the walks the two of us would take. He was always pausing to stare at things and figure out why they were behaving as they did, and I would stand there, only half listening as my mind veered off into a meditative state where I got absorbed by the patterns and colors and textures of the thing I was looking at and entered it with my imagination. We had loved our walks together for that reason, because each of us contributed such alien and fascinating perspectives on the world. Andy was already slipping in and out of consciousness when I finally got the diagnosis from the doctor and whispered it to him: one lone cancer cell from the bladder had escaped to the liver, and in just a few weeks his body was overwhelmed. I like to think he heard and was satisfied, for he died the next day.

What Andy was asking for was *cause*, which is different from *meaning*. You can know the cause of a disease or a weather event, but even the most conclusive scientific data fail to answer the metaphysical longing that can vex us when we're upended by tragedy. What's behind this? Why me? Why now? What if I had done this or that differently? Some people believe that they really are privy to the "sense" behind these big tragedies. Disaster is God's revenge for homosexuality or mineral extraction or women working outside the home. They're cosmic punishment for some unforgiven personal wrong. There are those who say that the coronavirus was engineered in a laboratory and loosed by villainous scientists upon an unsuspecting world. Or Bill Gates is behind it; he's inserted tiny transistors into the testing apparatus that will work their way into your blood and track your every movement. In the end, however relentlessly you search your memory and try to read the cosmic mind, you'll never get to the exact and singular deed that thrust you into your private hell.

Settling upon some underlying explanation for an event may bring temporary comfort, but it will never bring us any closer to dealing with life's big sorrows—or its joys. In the end, sense cannot be found in a senseless act. Life is random, capricious, horribly cruel at times, at other times insanely beautiful. It's a crap shoot. Roll the dice and get ready to be surprised. For Rob, it's this: You get on the lift to the ski slope and sit next to a woman who at first ignores your pleasantries, then agrees to have a drink with you, and a year later becomes your wife. For Mary it's this: The child you've so long awaited is born with a severe neurological disease and you end up having to feed and bathe and care for her for twenty-five years before she dies. Where is the "sense" in any of it? Life is constantly zapped with encounters, coincidences, and whimsies that shake the ground we're walking on and point us in new directions we could not previously have conjured for ourselves.

Can I bear to live with the utter pointlessness of so many of life's phenomena? Only if I toss aside the impossible project of demanding meaning from a meaningless situation and instead focus on devising the best way possible to move through it. Confronted with crisis, I must cease seeking the reason why and jump to the question of *Now what?* Sometimes the answer to that question is as simple as, *Do nothing right now. Simply sit in stunned paralysis.* That was frequently my only option in the first couple of weeks after Andy died. I would do some task like weeding the garden or shredding some of the voluminous files he'd saved for decades, and then all I could manage was to sit and stare, thinking nothing, planning nothing, until the next right act swam into my consciousness. Any suggestion that I ought to be devoting time to "making sense" of my husband's death would have been too much to bear. And really, would any of us, including survivors and grieving family members, feel any relief at all if the contents of a divine mind were suddenly revealed, and we learned the precise psychological prompting that convinced a bespectacled sixty-four-year-old real estate investor to kill all those people who had only wanted to gather together in a Las Vegas park to listen to music on a warm October night?

Almost always, in the moment, there is a thing you can do that makes sense. *Now*—in Ukraine, a child hears Russian missiles dropping nearby and is afraid to go to sleep. You sing to her. *Now*—half an hour before your friends are due to arrive for dinner, you drop the roast on the kitchen floor. You test the options: scavenge the cupboards or go to a restaurant? *Now*—you sit in the doctor's office waiting to learn the result of your latest biopsy. You note that, amazingly, you are breathing still and your breath will likely get you through the next minute and the one after that. The next right thing may seem very tiny and apparently insignificant, but it ushers you forward into the mystery.

4. Evolve mourning.

When she was young, my friend Liz loved a certain forest in New Hampshire. She spent long hours there, and her concept of God was wrapped up in her relationship with those trees—the way they bowed and righted themselves in the wind, the way they sheltered, shaded, withstood, accepted seasons and adapted to weathers. They consoled her when she was unhappy and exalted her when she was already upbeat. She was a teenager when a fierce storm blew into that forest, wiping out a large swath of trees. Liz was heartbroken. She had lost a friend, a spiritual presence, a guide. The next time her high school English teacher assigned the class an essay, she wrote about her love and grief for the forest. The teacher read the essay aloud to the class—not to praise it but to scorn it. When he finished reading, he chastised Liz for her sentimentality and her misguided notion that it was possible to love a mere *thing* like a forest. She was twice bereaved: once by the damage to her beloved forest and once by disrespect for her grief.

Cast your memory back to a place you've loved that's been cut down, paved over, poisoned, or ravaged by wind, water, or fire. Sink into the love you felt, and feel still, for that place. Face the solid fact of what has happened to wreck it and how that wreckage now hurts you. Find the place in your emotional body where love and grief meet. Is it a hole, a fire, the ash left after a fire, a scream, a sob? Whatever it looks or feels like, there at that place between love and grief is a knot that cannot be untied.

Yet if you, like Liz, have ever wept for the loss of a place or a being, you were probably told that you can't cry for the not-human. Maybe you've been told that you can't even love what isn't human. Maybe you, too, were mocked. Then, maybe, like Liz, you learned to keep quiet. It's time to rid ourselves of that ridiculous dogma. Global warming is warning us that we are going to lose a lot of things, living and nonliving, in the decades to come, and of course we feel sad about that. Now, thanks to the Australian philosopher and activist Glenn Albrecht, there's even a word to vindicate your feelings: *solastalgia*. *Solastalgia* means the "pain one feels when the place where one lives and that one loves is under assault." Albrecht has also defined it as "the homesickness you feel when you're still at home." Solastalgia legitimizes the psychological trauma of losing or being threatened with the loss of your place. Its symptoms, which Albrecht has also identified and named, include mermerosity, "a chronic state of being worried or anxious about the passing of the familiar"; topoaversion, "a feeling that you do not wish to return to a place that you have loved and enjoyed when you know that it has been irrevocably changed for the worst"; and terrafurie, "the extreme anger unleashed within those who can clearly see the self-destructive tendencies in the current forms of industrial-technological society, but feel unable to change the direction [of such activities]."[1] The concrete identification of these states of grief, disorientation, anxiety, helplessness, and stress from ecological loss has filled the gap between psychology and ecology. Solastalgia has inspired art exhibitions and songs and has become an important part of the testimony of plaintiffs fighting the encroachment of industrial-scale mineral exploitation on their land—and their well-being.

Maybe one reason it's so hard to admit our pain over the loss of a place is that it's even hard to admit our love of it. In his book, *The Mays of Ventadorn*, the poet W.S. Merwin describes a pivotal moment in his childhood. On a late afternoon during a visit he and his parents made to a friend's farm in northeastern Pennsylvania, the boy set off on a walk and found himself in a part of the land where he had never been before. Staring down into the valley and a line of trees that "curved like a wide river...toward the sun," he was transfixed. Merwin does not describe what he saw more fully. It was his own speechlessness in the captivity of awe that he remembered decades later. When he got back to the house, his mother asked him where he had been. "I tried to say something about the far valley I had seen, though I felt shy talking about it, as though it was a mistake to

20

say anything, and yet I wanted to tell them how beautiful it was, and I knew as I tried to that the words conveyed nothing at all about it."[2] What that boy, who would become a great poet, witnessed, and what he felt were too immense to shrink into words.

Yet, more and more, we are learning that nature has a great and complex intelligence which manifests in billions of ways, as those who have loved and mourned the non-human have intuitively known all along. As Henry Beston has written of animals, "They are not brethren, they are not underlings; they are other nations, caught with ourselves in the net of life and time."[3] Members of one of these great nations, elephants, grieve over their dead and continue to gather at the bony remains of a herd member long after the animal has died. Chimpanzees lean companionably together to watch a sunset from a high peak. Carl Safina describes an encounter with an orca whale possessed of either a sense of humor or a penchant for generosity. During an expedition to study the whales in British Columbia's Nootka Sound, a gust of wind blew the hat off the head of one of the passengers. A few moments later, an orca surfaced, the hat perched jauntily on its own head.[4]

Not just animals, but trees as well are experts in interpreting their environments and adjusting accordingly. Populating the thin, delicate tips of their roots are microscopic filaments of fungus that together create what is known as a mycorrhizal network, a highly successful, mutually sustaining partnership. The fungi consume about thirty percent of the sugar that trees take in through photosynthesis. Then, nourished and energized themselves, they scavenge the surrounding soil for minerals, such as nitrogen and phosphorus, that in turn feed the trees. Suzanne Simard, who has pioneered studies on arboreal communication, has discovered that the oldest, largest trees in a forest also act like nurses. They draw up water through their deep roots and make it available to younger seedlings. She has even shown that when neighboring trees are struggling, the great trees can detect their stress signals and increase the flow of nutrients accordingly.[5]

21

Even ice is alive to those who know it best. Author Robert Macfarlane told NPR radio host Rick Steves about the glaciers he encountered in Kulusuk, Greenland. These massive ice forms howl, sing, mutter, whip-crack, hum, and bang. They crash when they calve. They tick as they melt. They are constantly talking to themselves, and the villagers, who overhear them, have co-existed with them for many generations. But now, MacFarlane said, the glaciers have retreated so far away that they are silent. The people are no longer connected with them as they used to be, and they miss them deeply.[6]

Long before we had the scientific evidence of our kinship with other beings, we housed in our DNA awe, curiosity, and, yes, love of these mysterious beings who preceded us in life and kept to their own affairs while lacing in and out of ours. They are our ancestors and familiars, and we humans need to stay in proper relationship with them. A friend of mine from the Oneida Nation, whenever he sees a crow, lifts his hand in a casual wave of greeting. A Dineh (Navajo) man who was mourning a federal law that forced him to move off the high desert land where his family had lived for generations, said plaintively of the new territory that the federal government had decreed would be his new home, "The road won't know me." Once we were all indigenous and knew that we cohabited with different and exceptional intelligences. It's not just spiritually, but biologically true. Also residing in our DNA are the successful adaptations of all the generations that preceded us. One distant ancestor to whom we owe our very existence was a wormlike creature called *Ikaria wariootia*, who lived 550 million years ago.

Grief is essential to life and bound inextricably to love, and when what we love is taken from us, we mourn. Mourning is grief given expression. In the Mayan tradition, the spirits demand three offerings from their devotees: beauty, eloquence, and grief. Grief is their food, and when they don't get enough to eat, they get mad and start devouring humans. Martín Prechtel writes:

22

Grief is praise of those we have lost. Our own souls who have loved and are now heartbroken would turn to stone and hate us if we did not show such praise when we lose whom we love.... By the event of our uncontrolled grief, wail, and rap, we are also simultaneously praising with all our hearts the life we have been awarded to live, the life that gave us the health and opportunity of having lived fully enough to love deep enough to feel the loss we now grieve. To not grieve is a violence to the Divine and our own hearts and especially to the dead. If we do not grieve what we miss, we are not praising what we love.[7]

"What you know and love is finite. It is already slated for removal," writes Melissa Holbrook Pierson in *The Place You Love Is Gone.*[8] To tell someone that their grief for the loss of a nonhuman is inappropriate or stupid is to deny the depth and complexity of the emotional universe. If it were only people of the *homo sapiens* species that we were entitled to love, admire, be inspired by, and get deeply attached to, we would be poorer and simpler creatures in a diminished world. We would see our surroundings only as components of food and shelter, or tools for getting food and shelter, and we would cease to marvel. We would not give names to the dogs and cats who curl up beside us on the couch, delight us with their quirks, and comfort us when we're sad. We would not fall in love with a certain place and weep inconsolably when some climactic event that can no longer be considered a "natural" disaster flattens it. We are attached to our world, and it sticks to us, spooling around us and from us, like the sticky silk strands of a spider web. Of course we are in love. Of course we grieve.

We need to admit this love grief. Another wetland is plowed up and paved over for a fast food restaurant. Another ancient forest is decimated by saws or burned to cinders by wildfire. Pigs, chickens, sheep, and cows are maltreated during their short lives and killed without compassion, as if they were not living beings at all but commodities for consumption. And still the climate warms. Linda

Buzzell Saltzman and Sarah Anne Edwards point out that the grief we feel about the loss of nature is different from personal grief. "Grief that occurs after a loss usually ends with acceptance of what's been lost, and then one adjusts and goes on. But [environmental] despair is not a onetime loss that one learns over time to move on from. It's more like the process of accepting a degenerative illness— a chronic permanent state that will continue to worsen, probably for the entire lifetime of most people alive today."[9]

What will save us is that we do not have to grieve all by ourselves.

5. Resist the temptation to suffer alone.

I used to think I had the keys to triumphing over adversity: (1) never flinch from any reality, no matter what it is or how monstrous; (2) strive to do what has to be done in the best way possible; and (3) never let anyone know you're suffering.

The one part of that canon I got seriously wrong was the third. I thought plowing all alone through sorrow, doubt, difficulty, or fear was brave. Asking for help would be tantamount to handing my Sisyphean rock over to somebody else and lazing around while they shoved it up the mountain. Moreover, admitting to any emotion on the shadowy side of relentless determination would be to show weakness that others could take advantage of. I kept my problems to myself and so, without benefit of compassion or guidance, my isolation exacerbated my problems—a worsening condition which, naturally, I kept to myself. When the man I was in love with broke up with me at the end of our senior year in college, I never admitted even to my close friends how heartbroken I was. When he was killed in a motorcycle accident a year later, after we'd gotten back together, I walked the Boston streets by myself for hours, never letting anyone know that my body felt as crushed as his must have been by metal and asphalt. My logic revolved in a private circular argument. Because I suffered in silence, I viewed my suffering as special and unique; because I was special, I had to suffer in silence. I aspired to be one of those great and tortured authors who wrestled with mental illness: Virginia Woolf, Dylan Thomas, Anne Sexton, Sylvia Plath, Robert Lowell, William Faulkner. I also knew that if I didn't become as famous as they, I would face my disappointment alone and stoical.

It is not brave to suffer alone or exalted to achieve alone. The portrait of brave endurance that inspired my generation was advanced in the novels, comics, and TV shows we grew up with. The lone hero digs the bullet out of his own chest. He saves the poor widow from bandits. He rescues a horse from a burning barn. After accomplishing his brave deeds (the hero was always a man unless Lassie the dog was the star), he gallops off to his secret hideout without waiting to be thanked. He never sticks around long enough to fall in love or make friends, because attachments would distract him from his virtuous calling. This is not the picture of heroism that young people today aspire to. Today's superheroes conquer evil and save worlds by collaborating with their friends, who are not just sidekicks and fans, but individuals, each with their own particular skill that, somewhere along the trajectory of the plot, proves to be the exact one necessary to yank an amazing rescue out of the jaws of catastrophe.

Tori Heller, a young woman in her twenties whose job is educating youth in wilderness skills and appreciation, has been thinking about climate change for as long as she can remember. When she considers the doomsday scenarios that are not just possible but likely in her lifetime, being with friends and family is an essential part of her survival plan. "Maybe I'll have to live off the land," she told me, "gather my friends around me, and we'll deal with natural disasters. I feel like the only thing that really matters, if there was some catastrophe, if there was a war or climate disaster— all I'd want was for my friends and family to be in the same place with me." Living with climate change is a burden we must all bear. And yet, says the great educator and author Joanna Macy, that responsibility, that burden can be a spiritual path. "We are going to have to link arms to walk this path," Macy says in a documentary video by Anne Macksound and John Ankele, "because there are ditches on either side of us. One side is paralysis, shutting down because we feel too puny, too guilty, and too weak to see what's happening—or too victimized. And the other ditch is panic."[1]

Scientists, too, are rethinking decades of assumptions about how living beings best survive hard times. Biologist E.O. Wilson, who coined the term *biophilia*, the innate love that people have for nature, recently opposed the theory, most famously proposed by evolutionary biologist Richard Dawkins, that members of species with a "selfish gene," which favors their own survival over that of others, are more likely to progress to higher evolutionary states. To the contrary, says Wilson, cooperation works better.

The collaborative behavior of slime molds is a particularly intriguing example. For most of its lifetime, the slime mold *Dictyostelium* exists as a single-celled amoeba that lives in the soil, where it feeds on bacteria. But when food is in short supply, thousands of these individuals cluster together to form a body. The new conglomerate elongates into a slug-shaped mass that then begins to slither through the soil toward the light. When it reaches the surface, some of the cells form a stiff stalk, while others creep to the top of the stalk and metamorphose into spores. The spores then catch a ride on the feet of a passing animal until they drop off to start a new generation in a new place. It turns out that humans, like slime molds, ants (Wilson's own specialty), and honeybees, also function better when they are able to make a "wise collective decision." Yes, we do act selfishly under certain conditions, Wilson argues, but we also need to be part of and contribute to the collective. It's not braver and smarter to do every hard thing on your own. In fact, if we behave as if we must always prevail at the expense of others, we lose out. It's those who share and accomplish their goals together who are more likely to benefit.[2]

In his book about the *hibakusha*, victims of the atomic bomb that the U.S. dropped on Hiroshima, Robert Jay Lifton tells the story of a woman who was thirteen years old on that day when the sky flared, a mushroom-shaped plume swelled over the city, and people, trees, and buildings fried. Because of the exposure, this woman was disfigured by keloids, ropy scars etched into her skin from the burns of the blast. For years she felt so ugly and ashamed that she kept to herself. It was only when she joined a peace movement and began to associate with others that she felt once again that her life might have some meaning after all. She told Lifton, "For the first time I realized I was not alone in my suffering and that there were so many people who could understand us.... From the deep inspiration coming from those meetings I believe that my present self was born."[3]

Even as increasing numbers of people around the world have finally ceased to disbelieve in the reality of climate change, there are still some who think they can escape its ravages by moving to a safe mountaintop far inland from shrinking and tempestuous coastlines. That they will be immune is unlikely. As our global society discovered during the time of COVID, there are some phenomena from which none of us is exempt, whether we're a maid cleaning rooms in a hotel or a famous musician performing before thousands in a sports arena. In our physical isolation during the pandemic, we were determined not to retreat into social isolation. Instead, we gathered on Zoom for school, meetings, workshops, religious services, conferences, and yoga classes.[4] Many people attended these online events who would not have been able to come in person, and new relationships formed. A friend told me that, after attending a Twelve-Step program on line for several months, she sometimes couldn't remember which people she actually knew in person and which she had befriended through internet meetings.

You're trudging along your path in life, fussing about this and that, dreaming of how things could be, ought to be, deserve to be better, and all of a sudden an enormous boulder crashes down and blocks your way. It might be illness, the death of a loved one, a difficult child, heartbreak, unemployment, an unjust accusation, or any of a thousand other debilitating woes. Whatever the emergency, you get behind your rock and push, because what else can you do? And even as you're shoving that awful obstacle, absolutely preoccupied with it, believing your entire life depends on moving it at least somewhat out of the way, you have to attend to such mundane and vital things as making sandwiches for children, routing out some official document you haven't seen in years, holding the hand of an aging parent who no longer knows who you are, remembering to pick up some laundry detergent, or filling out

FEMA forms. The rock is the reality of what you've got. You don't deserve it, but you've got it, and so you push. You push your rock to the top of the mountain. However, contrary to what I once believed, you don't have to do it alone. Maybe no one else can take the burden away. The rock is yours to deliver to its mountaintop. But what you discover is that—*Oh!*—when you reach out, you find that others are glad to walk beside you, their hands laid gently on your shoulder.

6. Abandon hope.

Contrary to what you have been told, you don't need it to survive. Hope was the last ill to escape from Pandora's box, not because it could override all the other calamities that had already swarmed into the world, but because it was the trickiest sibling of them all. It had disguised itself as something other, something nicer and friendlier, but it was actually treacherous. For, truly, hope is subtle, sneaky, and shy. It doesn't ravage your body the way lust or jealousy or outrage does, having its way with you so violently that you can't ignore it. Rather, it creeps up on you and persuades you that things might not be so bad after all. Taken to extremes it tells you that it's fine to disbelieve in your reality.

I abandoned hope when I was twenty-six years old and my mother was dying of lung cancer. One day, her doctor sat down beside me in the hospital waiting room and told me not to lose hope. But I could see how she declined every day, and his advice infuriated me. There was no hope there. She was dying and, as far as I could see, he was telling me to overlook that certainty and pin my perspective of the future on a will-o-the-wisp. I determined that I would reject hope and deal with what was.

Is life possible without hope? If you give up hope, do you have to find something to take its place? If you send it packing, do you get to call it back in a desperate situation? And, if so, will it come? Or do you strive to live the best way you can without hope, because you realize that hope really isn't necessary for survival?

Hope is a ball of longing cast into the future. When I hope, I say, *I can't make things happen the way I want. Maybe somebody else can.* Yes, hope can be a motivator: you do what you must do now in order to launch projects and processes that others might then bring to fruition. On the other hand, hope can be an excuse to delay action: you do nothing, because (choose one): you don't know how, you don't have time, God will fix it, it's too big a task, it's beneath you, somewhere down the line there's bound to be a person or invention or event that takes care of things you can't. Hope, like fear, is future-oriented. Fear tells you that the future is going to be really bad. Hope convinces you that things may turn out all right after all.

At a critical time in her life author and political activist Barbara Ehrenreich railed against hope:

> I hate hope. It was hammered into me constantly a few years ago when I was being treated for breast cancer: Think positively! Don't lose hope! Wear your pink ribbon with pride! A couple of years later, I was alarmed to discover that the facility where I received my follow-up care was called the Hope Center. Hope? What about a cure? At antiwar and labor rallies over the years, I have dutifully joined Jesse Jackson in chanting "Keep hope alive!"—all the while crossing my fingers and thinking, "Fuck hope. Keep us alive."

Besides arguing that hope subverts reality, Ehrenreich insists that, when it is used to motivate people to triumph over a serious disease, it "may place an additional burden on the already sick or otherwise aggrieved." They worry that, if they lack hope, they might inadvertently be contributing to the progression of the illness, whereas people who are good at hoping are more likely to get better. "To be hope-free is to acknowledge the lion in the tall grass, the tumor in the CAT scan, and to plan one's moves accordingly," writes Ehrenreich.[1] In other words, look the worst in the eye.

Can we act without hope, simply because the actions we take are the right ones, the beautiful ones, the *desirable* ones? Can we say, in effect, *I may never again be happy, but meanwhile I will look out the window and look and look until I see something beautiful. I may not recover from this illness, but I will live each day with as much zest as I possibly can.*

My favorite example of taking right action without hope is the Norse myth of the Norns. These three sisters, like all the beings of that cosmology of grim complexity, live in the World Tree,

Yggdrasil. The gods have their domain, the dwarves theirs, humans theirs. Like the world we now inhabit, the World Tree is dysfunctional and fraught with danger. A stag tears at the leaves with his teeth. A squirrel named Ratatosk, scampers up and down the branches, inciting suspicion and spreading malicious gossip. A dragon gnaws at the roots. And everyone knows that the apocalypse, Ragnarok, is inevitable. One day the great wolf Fenrir will open his massive jaws and start devouring all that exists, starting with the sun. The Earth will tilt on its axis and civilization will lose its grounding. A war will begin and will end only with the total destruction of all.

And yet, the Norns have a job to do. They spend their days at the Well of Fate, dipping their hands into the water and mixing it with clay, then dabbing the salve they've made on the wounds of the tree. They hold out no hope that their lonely task will one day culminate in a rosier outcome. They don't tell themselves that someday somebody will figure out a solution. They neither implore nor blame the gods. And they don't deny the signs of reality eroding their world. Why do they do what they do with such regularity, such mindfulness, such devotion? They do it because it is their sacred work. They do it because not to do it would be to deny what they know is theirs to manage and care about. The right action does not depend upon having a right outcome. It depends on taking the action because that is the action that rises before you in the moment with all its grace and power and majesty—and because it demands to be done. The action is all.

Sometimes the action is inviting into your home a family you don't know who has lost everything in a wildfire and sometimes it is going for your next chemotherapy session. We do not need hope to do the thing that must be done. We need only recognize the singular call of what is before us and say *Yes* with all our might. Hope, then, is irrelevant. No one else can take this action. Only you, only now, in communion with what is before you.

II. PUNCH

I allow myself to sink to the bottom of my sorrow, but I can't stay there. After descending, not just once and for all, but as often as necessary, to reconnoiter with the hard reality of my situation, to rage and mourn, I must punch through the darkness into a little bit of light. To punch is to say both yes and no to my reality. It is acceptance of what is before me—and it is fierce resistance to being conquered by it.

This "punch" doesn't have to be some grand heroic action. The light I'm determined to grab, moreover, doesn't have to be so clear and brilliant that I know, upon seeing it, that I'll never again feel pain, and my path ahead will be happy, safe, and secure. Punching through the darkness, helplessness, and despair of hard times is, when it comes right down to it, just a matter of daring to move out of the place of stuckness. I must do this repeatedly, over and over, for idleness is a powerful convincer that doing nothing is all I'm good for. Without any guarantee—or any hope—that my forceful act will succeed, I move. I punch the stale air before me and open the way to freshness.

7. Punch through the avalanche.

The brother of a friend of mine escaped death by punching through an avalanche. Peter V. was skiing on a remote slope in Colorado when he heard the unambiguous rumble of a snowy mountain rapidly gaining on him. He had hardly begun to consider how to shift course when the ice-white force engulfed him. Pressed down and shoved forward by speeding snow, he recognized that all his athletic prowess and physical strength had suddenly become irrelevant. Death would be the outcome of this abduction. Accepting his new reality, he sank into the inevitability of his ending. Time gave him no opportunity to bypass the temptation to disbelieve.

Somewhat to his surprise, Peter realized that dying was not such a big deal after all. The snow slowed, halted. Quiet settled around him. So. Death had not come yet. Soon, though, it would, that he knew. What being hurtled down the mountain had not accomplished, suffocation would. He had no idea what was up or down, or how much snow surrounded him.

Suddenly he realized that he needed to live. So he took the only action left to him. He punched. He mustered all his force until he had freed his arm as much as possible, and then he punched straight ahead as hard as he could. With that gesture, he broke through his tomb of snow into air, sunlight, a snowy mountainside, and life.

If you were trapped in an avalanche, what would you do? Would you try to find meaning in your impending death? Would you weep cold tears as you awaited your demise? Would you pray? Would you punch? An Australian study identified three common responses to crisis: (1) fundamentalism, (2) nihilism, and (3) activism. The fundamentalist believes that the events of her life have been foreordained and are therefore inevitable. She has no choice but to acquiesce to the situation, because God has willed it. The nihilist sees the problem as a breakdown of social and moral orders and believes that the only possible solution is to take care of himself and his loved ones as best he can. The response of the activist is to act.[1]

Punching through the avalanche is the gesture of the third approach. The avalanches of our lives are not the kind that tumble down mountainsides. They're not even the problems that vex us from day to day. Instead, the avalanche I'm talking about is the passivity and helplessness that can so thoroughly engulf you when you're in the midst of a painful situation and feel like you're being pressed into a corner, your every escape route closed off. You can't get a breath of air, because all your air has been sucked into a great big bag of terror. It's all just too much to cope with. When you're struggling like that, you can easily slip into a conviction that doing little is doing enough, for you, you tell yourself, simply don't have the energy to do more, and no one should expect it of you. A sense of entitlement then begins to creep over you. It's almost as if you deserve your pitiful torpor. However, it is at this precise moment, when you are tempted to capitulate and call it being good to yourself, that you really need to punch. The avalanche is a state of mind. You punch out of it in the moment you realize that if you don't, you could cower there indefinitely.

Wallace Stevens wrote: "After the final no there comes a yes / And on that yes the future world depends."[2]

Sometimes punching out of the avalanche is a huge, bold move, like Peter V's. Usually it's smaller. Maybe punching out of the avalanche is turning off the TV that you've been slouched in front of all afternoon—a time when you would ordinarily be at work and aren't now, because you got laid off when the coronavirus pandemic hit—and calling a friend or going outside for a walk. A study published by the American Psychological Association's PsychNet and released during the pandemic showed that aerobic exercise significantly reduced depression, anxiety, and stress.[3] If outside exercise seems too big a risk to take during self-isolation, said Kathleen McIntyre, who led the study, tuning in to an online workout or playing actively with children is a good alternative. In fact, just about any forceful punch out of passivity can help. New York City residents who threw open their windows at 7:00 PM each day throughout the spring of 2020 to join neighbors in cheering the city's health care workers, said they ducked back inside a few minutes later feeling a sense of solidarity, gratitude, and even happiness. The wall of powerlessness crumbled as they shouted out their appreciation of others, with others. Ah! It turns out you can breathe after all. It turns out you have at hand an action that, when you do it, changes you. You are alive. And, just possibly, you can get through this.

For Greta Thunberg, the punch could hardly have looked less like the decisive, world-changing action it turned out to be. When she realized at the age of eleven what climate change meant for all living beings on the planet, Thunberg became severely depressed. She spoke only to her family and to one teacher. She wouldn't eat outside her home. She didn't emerge from this grief until, at age fifteen, she determined that there was one simple thing she could do: she could station herself in front of the Swedish Parliament with a sign demanding that the government take action to address climate change. She began skipping school on Fridays and sitting on the steps of the building with a hand-made sign that read, "Climate Strike." That was her first punch. She took the second one on the day a stranger approached and offered her a dish of take-out vegetarian pad thai. Contrary to her habit, she ate it. Things began to change. Other young people joined her at the Parliament. By the end of that year, tens of thousands of school students across Europe were skipping school on Fridays to protest their own governments' failure to act. Now, says Thunberg's father, she has come to life. "She dances around, she laughs a lot, we have a lot of fun—and she's in a very good place."[4]

This young girl, who became *Time* Magazine's Person of the Year in 2019, had come to the realization that the only possible action before her was to punch. Because she has Asperger Syndrome, a form of high-functioning autism characterized by difficulty with social skills and an exceptional ability to concentrate on a single subject, Thunberg's form of punching would not be loud and public. Nor would it would entail enlisting a lot of other people to join her. (The reason so many did just that later on was that they were inspired by her.) The sign she lettered by hand was her voice. Her resolute, now world-famous, scowl was her invitation to the rest of the world to pay attention—not to her but to her cause. Her decisive act to reclaim life did not occur on the day somebody joined her at the parliament. It was when she stepped out of her house with her sign.

My first big punch out of the avalanche of Andy's death was brought on by a storm. About a week and a half after he died I was out mowing the lawn when the sky darkened and the wind began to whip and whirl. Even though it was summer, leaves and twigs flew out of the trees to twirl in the air. Since our house was the last one in the village before the countryside opened up, we often lost power in severe storms, and it seemed likely that that could happen in the storm that was shaping up now. I finished mowing the lawn and had just gone inside when, sure enough, the lights flickered and went dark, the old refrigerator gave a last choking gasp, and the house settled into premature silence and darkness. I went upstairs to take a shower before the hot water cooled, and then I went into the bedroom and sat on the bed. Through the windows I could see the rain driving almost horizontally from the west, the tops of the trees slapping back and forth. Suddenly, the violence of the tempest mirrored my own violent anguish so sharply that I felt I must be on the verge of death myself, for I could not possibly live much longer with such pain. It seemed that grief itself was about to extinguish my own life, just as the storm had shut off the power in our house.

Andy and I had always told each other that we wouldn't want to live if something happened to the other. Now, though, sitting on our bed, as the storm crashed over our home and over me, I realized that I didn't want to die, and I rebelled. "I want to live!" I wailed. "I want to live! Show me," I pleaded to whatever great force might hear and intervene, "show me how to survive this!"

My grief did not lessen after that imploring plea, but something changed. I came into an unexpected rendezvous with my own fierce consciousness, and realized that, actually, I would survive. I still tumbled into moments of anguish every day, but my declaration to the cosmos that I wanted to live gave me the courage to stick with the suffering as much I had to in order to come out on the other side.

I wish life afforded more opportunities to get so decisively out of a bad situation as punching out of a mound of snow that will suffocate you in a few short minutes if you don't act fast. It's usually not like that. How do you know when it's time to bust loose and when you should just lumber on with the hardship at hand? When is it advisable to be like Peter, punching as hard as he could the moment the snow stopped, and when is the best option the way of Sisyphus, shouldering his rock yet again? Sisyphus shoves his rock up a mountain. Peter got rolled down a mountain by a roaring engine of snow. Sisyphus has to fetch his burden time after time and maneuver it back to the summit, even though he knows he can never, for all eternity, make it stick there. Peter, during those seconds when he was being catapulted down the slope, also had no expectation that his ball of trouble would ever arrive at a place stable enough to permit him to escape his fate. He faced imminent death; Sisyphus faces eternal life. Both Peter and Sisyphus must come to terms with the real horror of never walking out of their current circumstances. And yet they do. They both punch through the avalanche, because neither stays put in his misery, waiting for some outside force to come along and rescue him just because he is, or thinks of himself as, a decent human being. Both of them rouse themselves out of submission to inertia and shove with all their might. The shove, that gesture out of snow or behind a rock on a steep incline, marks the beginning of the end of powerlessness. And after the punch, you may find yourself emboldened to do something even more daring.

38

8. Dare.

Courtney Miles was eighteen years old and living in New Orleans on boredom and handouts. He had stopped going to his high school classes and spent most of his time on a neighborhood basketball court. When he went home, it was to squat in the abandoned house of his mother, who was in jail for dealing drugs. His father lived in another city. He scrounged for food where he could. On Thursday, September 1, 2005, as Hurricane Katrina started bending trees and hurling objects into the streets, he was walking around the neighborhood with his friends, just checking things out. Then water from the city's overwhelmed levees started coursing through the streets and suddenly, Courtney Miles had a completely unprecedented thought. He realized that people were going to need help and he knew how to give it. They would go to the bus station, he told his friends. They'd each get in a bus, and then they'd drive around the city and pick people up.

The bus depot was deserted because of the storm, but they found a box of keys. Commandeering eight buses, they set out in different directions, collecting stranded people. Miles couldn't leave anyone behind. "I was already full," he told a reporter later. "They were running toward the bus, smacking the windows. So I was like, 'Just get in where you fit in.'" Some of the renegade drivers took their passengers all the way to Houston, where shelters were being set up. Miles headed to Lafayette, a hundred and fifty miles away. When he arrived at the shelter, he wolfed down a slice of pizza, then turned around and drove straight back to New Orleans, this time supplied with a gas credit card donated by a stranger. In the end, he rescued about four hundred people. He worried that he might be arrested for stealing a bus, but in fact he was hailed as a hero. "Whether it's right or wrong, I felt it was right," he said. [1]

Miles dared to do something completely original, unplanned and, his friends and former teachers might have said, uncharacteris-

39

tic. Leaping from lethargy into action, from struggling to preserve his own life to igniting his friends, he dared, and changed the course of many lives, including his own.[2] He heard the siren call of a really good idea, and he answered *Yes!* A plan had burst upon him: that driving around in city buses was a way to save desperate people. He punched when he voiced this good idea to his friends. The dare we take that shifts the ground in a tough situation isn't the taunt your friends nudged you with when you were a kid: *Dare you to stick your tongue on that icy pole.* It's not the kind of dare that could endanger you or lure you into doing something unethical: *I dare you to steal a six-pack of beer from the deli.* And although this inner prompt calls you to an urgent corrective, it is rarely as newsworthy as saving four hundred lives, or even one life. You might dare, for example, to finally call the credit card company and ask for a lower interest rate on the balance that's been mounting every month. That might sound like a small thing, but it's a difficult one nonetheless. You have to admit powerlessness and ask for help. Accepting the dare and making the call frees you up, gives you a plan, and enlists somebody else into the project of helping you move your life in a different direction. Daring is doing the thing you're a little reluctant to do but very much want to do. It shifts the trajectory not just because it turns a key in outer circumstances, but also because it makes you realize you're not powerless after all, that you can take actions that make a difference. Daring is different from punching out of the avalanche. Punching out of the avalanche is the action that propels you out of inaction. Daring is the action that clears the path to the next action. For Courtney Miles, the punch was when he and his friends turned their footsteps toward the bus station. Accepting the dare was getting those keys out of the box, turning the ignition, and setting off into the flooding streets of New Orleans.

Of course, we would usually rather postpone accepting the dare, even if it's we ourselves who are proposing it. Doing that bold, outrageous thing would demand too much of us! We have too many other things to worry about! Courtney Miles, who was young and

Black and a school dropout, was afraid he'd be punished for what he risked doing. In times of stress and sorrow, saying yes to the dare that crooks its finger at you from within your very being can feel like a gargantuan task. *What if it doesn't work? What if they laugh at me? What if I get in trouble? Maybe I'll do it tomorrow.* But when we follow that subtle, sometimes blurry guidance, we almost always find that it leads to a new freedom .

The philosopher Lewis Gordon has pointed out that the word "existence" comes from the Latin *existere*, combining *ex* (from) and *sistere* (to take a stand). *Existence* actually means "to stand out." Each of us goes through daily life surrounded by our background—parents, race, ancestral trauma, a community, a predilection for a certain style of clothing, a disability, a preoccupation of the moment—and through our actions we *stand out* from that background. We respond to it or turn our backs on it, we rely on it to guide us or we rebel determinedly against it. "Standing out" does not mean showing off or becoming famous; it means daring to claim our existence by determining our actions as consciously and meaningfully as we possibly can. Standing the ground we stand on, we give ourselves shape and agree to stand out.

In his work, Gordon, who is African American, shows how a Black person's background makes demands that are different from those of a white person, for their whole lifespan is bound up in cultural prejudice, disparagement, distrust, and low expectations. In his act of daring, then, Miles was taking a much bigger risk than a white person in the same circumstances, since the law in America is inclined to suspect Black people of misdemeanors far more readily than they do white people. In times of suffering, it can take immense courage to decide to stand out, for suffering makes us vulnerable and tells us that it is safer to react not boldly but with special caution.[3] In his *Book of Calamities* Peter Trachtenberg refers to the work of Simone Weil, who pointed out that people who have endured great suffering become mere *things* to themselves. "The 'I' within them is crushed,"[4] writes Trachtenberg. The psyche tells you that if you're used to being rejected, admonished, shut out, then your response is very likely to be, *If I am nothing, then I deserve nothing.* That is why the stories of people like Courtney Miles make such an impact: they remind us that even when we're crushed, we are capable of great courage. A dare we give ourselves and then accept makes us *stand out* in ways that can have profound consequences. Even when they have no apparent consequences at all, those dares we accept are nonetheless very important to us, as the person who makes them, for they signal our refusal to capitulate to being a victim and instead assert, *I am something!* Daring is not guaranteed to save a life, but it almost always saves the moment.

9. Do it because only you can.

One morning in 2016, lawyer and former gymnast Rachel Denhollander read an article in the *Indianapolis Star* reporting that The United States of America Gymnastics (USAG) organization had been covering up claims of sexual abuse by coaches. In her book *What Is a Girl Worth?*, Denhollander recounts the action she took next, which would upend her life and spotlight the way sports organizations systematically overlooked sexual abuse to shield their reputations. She put down the newspaper, went to her computer and, while bouncing her baby on her lap, typed:

" 'I am emailing to report an incident…. I was not molested by my coach, but I was molested by Dr. Larry Nassar, the team doctor for USAG. I was fifteen years old.' " She continues: "I paused for a second. I knew exactly what it would mean for me and my family if the *Indy Star* decided to pick up the story. I'd known for years what the cost would be. But it had to be done, and if it wasn't done now, it might never happen." She ended her letter with the words, " 'I have seen little hope that any light would be shed by coming forward, so I have remained quiet. If there is a possibility that is changing, I will come forward as publicly as necessary.' " [1]

Denhollander had no idea when she wrote that email what would happen. She just knew she had to do it and that she, with her experience of Nassar's abuse, aggravated by years of helpless outrage afterwards, was the one person capable at that moment of doing what had to be done. Her willingness to tell her story emboldened many other women to come forward and describe Nassar's crimes against them when they were young athletes under his reputedly excellent medical care. None of them could have known when they told their stories publicly that Nassar would be tried and sentenced to sixty years in prison or that dozens of other officials from USAG, the United States Olympic Committee, and Michigan State University, where Nassar also worked, would be charged or fired.

They just knew they had to do it. They took an action as if their lives depended on it.

Each of them stepped to the cliff edge of their radical freedom and leaped. "Radical freedom" is the term Jean-Paul Sartre coined to elucidate his conviction that, although we can't choose or even control our circumstances, we can and must accept the responsibility of determining our response to those circumstances. For Sartre, that was the essence of existentialism, the philosophical movement he founded in Paris in the 1940s and that gained popularity during and after World War II, as people awoke to the horrors of Nazi concentration camps and the apocalyptic reality of the nuclear bomb. Existentialism reminded people that, no matter what challenges they faced, no matter how helpless they felt to effect change, they always had a choice to act. Moreover, that how they acted utterly defined who they were as humans.

Here's an extreme example of how the possibilities of radical freedom might present themselves. I'm standing on a street corner waiting for the light to change. Now, I have all kinds of radical choices of what to do in the interim: (a) punch the stranger next to me, (b) dash out in front of a bus to pick up a dime I spot lying in the street, (c) start singing the "Ode to Joy" at the top of my lungs, or (d) just stand there waiting for the light and thinking about what I'll have for lunch. Both the manner of choosing and what I choose can be critically important. Will I choose out of boredom? Habit? A yen for adventure? Altruism? Lust? The fifteen minutes of fame I've yet to achieve? Each choice I make is rooted in the moment and offers pathways that will shape my life and possibly the lives of others as well. In the far more likely situations and options that present themselves many times each day, I feel more able to take the most fiercely conscious of the paths that beckon when I remember that, of all the humans in the world, at that very moment and in those very circumstances, I am the only person capable of doing what calls to be done.

Before she even knew whether or not her home had survived

the Valley Fire that roared through Middletown, California in September 2016, killing three people and destroying more than five hundred houses, Sage Abella knew how she was going to respond. She would offer art classes to help people cope with the losses. Eleven days after the fire, she began teaching two classes for children and one for adults. Her goal was to encourage people to express what they felt both about the burned land all around them and the desolate emotional landscape within.

The classes were loosely organized. People could come and go at any time, a schedule easy on those who were so traumatized they often found it difficult to concentrate. One woman was so distraught that she sat sobbing while others painted. Finally she got a piece of paper and went into garden. There she became engrossed in trying to recreate the exact color of a rare lotus that had bloomed in her own garden before the fire. A veteran of the Iraq war filled his truck with supplies and brought them to town, then stayed to talk to people about post-traumatic stress. A woman who barely spoke made a painting eight feet high. *The ash is the medicine,* Sage realized one day as she picked up a chunk of charred gray pine. She began suggesting to her students that the ash itself could be a medium for their art.

Can we find a sense of purpose in the crises of our lives? Can we offer meaning and purpose to others, even as we ourselves stumble? And will we dare to take the actions that only we can take, because they present themselves to us as imperatives that grip the heart and ignite fire in the spirit? The environmental activist Vandana Shiva has said, "We need to wake up to the problems in the world and yet not get overwhelmed by the magnitude of them… not suffer in our activism, but instead find joy in what we are doing to help ameliorate the global problems."[2] With each decision, each act, each Yes, we carve out who we are.

10. Release the old reality.

In the supermarket I wasn't paying attention and pushed my cart into the back of the legs of a man walking in front of me. I hate it when somebody does that, and I apologized extravagantly to him and assumed that was that. But fifteen or twenty minutes later, I was pondering my choices of items on a shelf when my cart was suddenly rammed. I turned around and it was that same man, taking his opportunity to exact his revenge and now striding victoriously down the aisle. I had to laugh. He had carried his sense of injustice around all that time, and finally he got me.

Disbelieving reality means refusing to look squarely at a problem I have to deal with. Another form of disbelieving reality is refusing to acknowledge a contrary truth: that things *have* changed and that, by stubbornly sticking to the old reality or my own investment in it, I abdicate my creative response to life. Nothing in our collective modern lifetime has taught us so insistently as the coronavirus pandemic how reality can radically shift. You thought you'd be launching a certain project at work, and then you had to postpone it indefinitely or figure out how to do it online. You thought you were going to start your freshman year in college, and then you learned you'd be attending your classes on Zoom sometimes and from your dorm room sometimes, and then they announced that you could go to class in person after all, but you had to wear a mask, and then one of the students got COVID and you were sent home. You didn't know if you'd be able to find toilet paper (or sponges or pasta or peanut butter) in the grocery store, so you had to abandon the menu plan you made that morning and come up with something new that corresponded to what was on the shelves. You couldn't have coffee with friends, go to the dentist, see a movie, or visit your grandchildren. Then you were told it would okay to start being a little bit normal again, but the infection rates spiked even higher, because some people still disbelieved in the virus and refused to wear masks or get the vaccine, so you went back to isolating at home. The coronavirus catapulted us into living day by day, situation by situation, and learning to release the old realities of what was possible or necessary, either in our physical life or in our minds. We learned that brooding in a past reality often meant we were unprepared to act quickly and decisively in the present one.

One week after the murder of eighteen-year-old Michael Brown by a white police officer in Ferguson, Missouri, Dr. Marty K. Casey founded the Show Me Arts Academy to provide young people with a safe place to come and express their feelings through art, music and theatre. She later created UnGUN Institute to work with Black families who have been hurt by gun violence. Violence creates trauma in the body, Marty told me, like invisible bullets that keep wounding their victims over and over and preventing them from living a full, free life. "You need to defuse those trauma bullets," she said. "You don't need them! UnGUN them! Let them go!"

The past does cling, no doubt about it, and that is especially true when you've been hit by trauma. The big events of our past shape our reactions to present events. If you were repeatedly criticized as a child or if you nearly died in a car crash as an adult, that bruising impact on your body and your mind keeps slamming you long afterwards. But, oddly, the human psyche seems actually to welcome an opportunity to keep getting triggered by small and ordinary incidents as well, as that man in the supermarket apparently fumed at me for bumping into him until he could get me back. We not only allow some incident to clang on and on in our psyche long after the causal action has stopped, but actually encourage it to do so. I myself have brooded over broken friendships for months and even years until realizing, finally, that I had to pluck myself up and acknowledge the loss and just get on with it. Resentments, bitterness, and hurt aggravate way beyond their expiration date. We replay them over and over, as if reeling repeatedly from that blow justifies our sense of righteous victimhood. Releasing the old reality means being acutely attentive to the requirements of *now*. Peter V. would not have been able to punch out of the avalanche if he'd attempted that move while the snow was hurtling him down the mountain, but if he hadn't acted mere seconds later, he would have suffocated to death. A more mundane example: when you're stopped at a red light and the light turns green, you don't sit there in your car fretting about how traffic lights always make you late. You go.

Here is a true story from the coronavirus pandemic that illustrates how reality shifts from moment to moment and necessitates new choices of response. Cepani Harjo is a registered nurse in Islip, Long Island, New York. As COVID-19 gained its foothold over his life at work and at home, he started keeping a journal, excerpts of which were published in the HIMSS (Healthcare Information and Management Systems Society) online newsletter in April 2020. Those of us who aren't medical professionals assume that doctors and nurses must be acutely aware of how rapidly a patient's condition can change, so they'll be prepared to treat any shift in the condition. Here we can also see how Harjo's very personal emotional responses blend with the medical details he must attend to:

> I feel as though I'm swimming with my clothes on just trying to do my ordinary nursing tasks. The plastic gown has a suffocating feel to it and I start sweating beneath it within a few minutes. My glasses fog as the N95 diverts my humidified breaths upward. As the day progresses, humidity accumulates in the mask making it harder to draw breaths. A test that took a few minutes takes 15 now.

> I get my first vent patient, a 70-year-old female who is not doing well. The ventilator becomes unattached twice while caring for her. The ventilator spews the humidified infected air of the infected patient briefly into my surrounding environment and I fear possible exposure.

> [The family of another patient] wants to visit but they are not allowed. The best we can do for now is hold a cell phone

to the patient's ear. "We love you so much. Hang in there. Miss you Mom, Gamma, honey." I clean and turn her, fix her hair and turn to leave the room fighting off tears.

The nurses in the [Emergency Department] are so overwhelmed that they have not the time to fetch a patient a sip of water.

Another patient arrives on a stretcher. His rhythm is bradycardic, slow, in the 40 beats-per-minute range as I feel for a pulse that is not there. I pull the code bell and start doing chest compressions on his chest. The attending physician, a cardiologist I recognize, swings around the corner and shouts to stop because the patient was coded three times in the ED. Thanks for the present.

At home I drop my shoes outside in the back porch and wave to my two sons and wife in the living room from the kitchen. I make a beeline to the bathroom, drop my clothes on the floor and sterilize myself from head to toe. After I wrap the towel over my work clothes and walk straight to the basement and drop them in the washing machine and start it.

I walk upstairs, wash my hands again, pour myself a beer and say hello again to my people who are watching a movie in front of a warm fire. They slide to the other side of the couch as I sit with a thud, beyond exhausted. No hugs, no kisses for now. I sleep alone on the couch in the living room, uncomfortably waiting for my next shift.[1]

Discomfort, fear, compassion, fatigue, annoyance, and sadness lace Harjo's account. His every interaction is a push-pull experiment with who he is, what his world is throwing at him, and what he does with all that material. He is a nurse. He brings years of professional skill to his work. He knows how to handle an emergency, but now he finds himself in a whole new kind of emergency, and he's not always sure how to respond. He is compassionate; he stifles his tears as he fixes the hair of the woman who can't be with her loving family as she dies. He gets irritated at the cardiologist who has neglected to tell him that their patient has already died. He chafes inside his uncomfortable protective gear. And, perhaps hardest of all, when he gets home after an exhausting day of work, he feels unwelcome. His family scooches over to the far end of the couch so as not to get too close to him.

Harjo's story magnifies the constant interplay with our environment that we all engage in every day and how we are continually being called to release the attitudes and actions of the moment before and activate new ones. For most of us, daily realities are not so dramatic and certainly not so critical to the very existence of others. Still, like Harjo, we feel constant streams of ever-new demands caressing and pummeling us throughout the day. Every moment is brand new and demands a new and apt response. Lingering in the past just muffles our ability to move forth in the present. We are all comets, burning through space on our way to the sun, as the solar winds warm, taper, and elongate us. We are actors and acted upon. Surviving hard times means being attuned to shifts of circumstance so that we can respond with grace, grit, and creativity to what is demanded in the now, rather than dragging around a bag of old reactions and constantly re-engaging with them. Watch the leaf on an aspen tree. When the wind blows, it shimmies wildly. When the wind stops, the leaf stills. It does not keep fluttering in order to remind itself of its own great capacity for movement, or so that it will be prepared for when the next wind comes. It releases the old reality. It responds to what is. It stills.

11. Sing through the darkest night.

During the decades of apartheid in South Africa, when many Black inmates at Pretoria Central Prison were executed for their political activities, they knew their time was up when they were marched from their regular cell in the maximum security prison to a special section known as "The Pot." That was where those sentenced to die would spend their last seven days. They had been arrested because they fought against laws and social constraints that had reduced them to servants and suspects in their own country. Now their life was unspooling rapidly to its end and, as far as they knew, their efforts to change those policies of oppression had been fruitless.

Yet there was a practice in The Pot that, if it could not counter the despair, did exploit and then explode it. Often on the last night of his life, as he awaited the dawn of his death, a condemned men would begin to sing. Then the men in the adjoining cells would add their voices to the chorus. All of them in that cell block knew they would be dead within just a few days, and yet they sang, and their voices filled the darkness. One former prisoner, Robert McBride, recounted: "The miracle is that they are far apart and it takes time for sound to travel and yet there's complete harmony. It would be wrong to say it's beautiful, but it is. It's horrible beauty. It's almost paranormal the way things are. I used to just sit on my table with my feet on my bed, listening, smoking. It was very funny business. Even when a guy had been crying, he'd stop crying and sing."[1]

A "horrible beauty" he called it. Singing in the face of tribulation was an act of horrible beauty, because it both acknowledged the grief, loneliness, and powerlessness, and addressed that condition with voices rising together. Could it be that these men had the secret of how to greet death—or, in fact, any great human trial? Knowing that the iron door of the cell will creak open in the morning, not for freedom, but for the last walk you'll ever take—nevertheless, now, you sing. You bring forth the music of your heart. You sing both your life and your death. You sing out all those you've loved and your grief for having to leave them. You sing for all the sweetness and struggle you've seen and will see no more. You sing because singing moves you out of your own tears. It moves you not out of your sorrow but so deep down into it that you pass right through the personal and into the universal human condition of sorrow. You must sing because if you don't sing, you'll die before you are killed. You sing because the end of your existence is near—but it has not yet arrived, and meanwhile you live. And, by god, you will keep right on living until you die.

To live fully in a time of crisis and anxiety is to cement ourselves in the moment and respond as if our whole being depends upon what we are doing right now. Slammed by bad news, heartbreak, loss, our response is likely to be—and appropriately so—fear and grief. Yet the life force still surges within us, as strong as ever, and when we can grab hold of it, we triumph. When we can sing or, even better, join others in the music of rebellious, stubborn, persistent life, we triumph together. That is why, during the first few weeks of the COVID pandemic, so many people all around the world were inspired by the smartphone videos of Italians emerging from confinement in their apartments to stand on their balconies and make music together. We all knew the grim statistics: that Italians were dying from the virus at a higher percent per capita than in any other country and that lockdown regulations were strictly enforced. Yet people could sing. From professional opera singers to amateur drummers, from "Volare" blaring out of a stereo across an apartment complex courtyard with all the neighbors joining in, to a lone violinist playing a sonata that brought listeners to tears, the Italians seized life and wouldn't let go. Their music-making didn't make the crisis go away, it didn't cure anybody, but it did, for a few minutes, ease the emotional pain and flip sorrow and anxiety into exuberant camaraderie with neighbors, family, country, and all paths to survival.

The singing I'm talking about here doesn't have to mean making music with the voice. Maybe it's dancing or wild play or twirling around in your back yard with your face upturned to the sky during a summer rain. As one young Italian man put it as he perched on the railing of his balcony, "Maybe in this moment there's the need to yell, to make noise, to take anything we have and find our vibration, our melody, communicate, transform what we're living individually and collectively."[2] Singing wildly in the dark means letting go of thought, planning, or the worry that somebody might be looking on with disapproval—and just joining in. Shaking the body and raising the voice catapults us into what Barbara Ehrenreich describes, in *Dancing in the Streets* as the ability to "acknowledge the miracle of our simultaneous existence with some sort of celebration."[3]

On January 10, 2021 my organization, Radical Joy for Hard Times, produced a Global Day of Mourning to commemorate the one-year anniversary of the death of a sixty-one-year-old man from Wuhan, China, the first officially declared fatality from COVID-19. We invited people to take a break from all the demands of coping and adapting and just surviving that the pandemic forced on us and pause to reflect on what the past months had meant to them, what they had lost, and what had pleasantly surprised them. The online series of events began with my conversation with Francis Weller, author of *The Wild Edge of Sorrow* and other books on moving through grief, and Dr. Marty K. Casey, founder of UnGUN Institute, helping Black youth to heal from the trauma of violence through the arts. We then offered five online "sharing circles," closed Zoom breakout groups during which people could come together and talk about what they were mourning and how they were coping. An elder of the Oneida Nation, Artley Skenandore, presented an Encouragement Ceremony, traditionally called a Condolence Ceremony and offered as a way to help grieving family members and friends dry their tears and step forth into "bright new footprints." Finally, we had a dance. For one hour, Daryl Henderson, a young fashion photographer and DJ from California, played music to usher people through the journey from sorrow to joy. Some people joined in on Zoom, while many others watched and danced on the live Facebook broadcast. The momentum of the music and the exuberant company gradually infused us until it was the dance that was moving the dancers. People were dancing with funny hats and stuffed animals they grabbed, and they were embellishing their images with silly internet filters of haloes and hearts and oversized glasses. We were in Ireland and California, Washington, DC and Texas, but we were dancing together, playing together, releasing pent-up emotion together. The sorrow of the past year was still a reality, but our bodies took in the music and swished it around with the sorrow until both those strains mingled like sugar in a cup of bitter tea.

If a group of men imprisoned only because they were fighting for their freedom can sing through the night before an execution, then any of us can sing (or dance) whenever the world is too much with us. When the highs and the lows come together, we can sing all night in the darkness.

12. Fight the angel—and let her win.

In a poem translated as "Man Watching," that begins with his reflection on an approaching storm, Rilke widens his focus to consider the immense forces that hammer and rearrange humans, just as the wind whips trees and beats down grasses. If we focus on fighting the small things, the poet writes, we claim proportionately small victories. However, if we grapple with more powerful foes, we may not win the battle, but we garner, in the process, some of our opponent's strength, vitality, and even majesty. Rilke considers the angel that biblical Jacob fought. There they were, angel and man, tussling at the foot of the ladder to heaven. Surely the angel could have made a quick end to the match and the man, but that didn't happen. Jacob was persistent and the angel, it seems, was more intent on teaching than inflicting a quick TKO. What Jacob wanted from the confrontation was no silver cup of champions. "I will not let you go till you bless me," he rages in the biblical telling. Winning, Rilke concludes, does not tempt the one who wrestles angels: "This is how he grows: by being defeated, decisively, / by constantly greater beings."[1] Rilke exhorts us to consider the foes that challenge us and throw the gauntlet only to the ones we're sure we want to engage, the ones we can learn something from, the ones whose mythic enormity we need to claim for ourselves. The ones that will bless us.

"Pick your battles, man" was the message that showed up in Donald Trump's Twitter feed two months after he won the 2016 election. Trump had taken to his favorite social media site to complain about Alec Baldwin's portrayal of him on *Saturday Night Live*, and a woman named Danielle Muscato took him on. "Jesus fucking Christ, @realDonaldTrump. You are the president-elect. Pick your fucking battles, man. You're embarrassing yourself." No doubt Rilke would have agreed with Muscato that Trump was putting a lot of effort into trying to triumph over a very small thing. As for Muscato herself, she was battling not so much with Trump himself as with the indignity he was foisting upon the high office he was about to attain. She surely had no hope of convincing Trump to stop tweeting his indignation, but she kept up her barrage of retorts for several hours and garnered the support of thousands of followers.

Who is the angel you've been avoiding and will now engage in battle? Maybe it's grief, long delayed. You've tried to put it out of your mind and out of your life, but now it insists that you meet it at the foot of the ladder to heaven and put up your dukes and save yourself. Another powerful angel is fear. We can easily imagine that Jacob was afraid when he woke up to find a great celestial being hovering over him. But he went ahead and engaged anyway, he didn't just curl up cowering in anticipation of the holy smiting. Fear tells me that getting involved is too big a responsibility. It tells me I'm not ready or that, if I do step in and undertake this large, scary thing, I'll die. Fear is normal. But when I find myself procrastinating or making excuses, chances are fear is the angel I need to wrestle with.

Fear brought a women named Sibyl to a wilderness rites of passage program for women that I led in the canyons of southeastern Utah. Although she was a successful psychotherapist in her forties, she had pushed aside the most painful subject of her own life: the sexual abuse she had endured from her father during the years of her childhood and adolescence. She had kept promising herself that one day she would deal with it. Now the time had come. The program entailed three days of preparation, during which the participants clarified their intentions and let go of an object symbolizing any past beliefs or attitudes that could get in their way of devoting themselves to those intentions. They then embarked on a four-day solo during which they fasted, drinking only water, and slept under a simple tarp. They also fasted from company and distractions like reading, and technology. After the solo, everyone came back to base camp and told the story of what they had experienced. Then we spent a couple of days doing a variety of exercises to help them incorporate the lessons and insights they'd gained into their lives back home.

When Sibyl returned on that morning after the solo, her whole face looked different. Before, there had been a pinched look about her. Now she shone, as if her whole psyche had been washed clean. The next day, she began her story by saying that, when she arrived at her solo spot in a hollowed-out half-bowl of a canyon wall, a small snake had been curled up right in the middle of it. She screamed. She hated snakes. Not sure if this one was dead or alive, she poked at it with a stick. The snake stirred, but did not move. She remembered my counsel to the group that the specific place that each person chose as her solo spot would guide and inform her experience, and she decided to sit with the snake, partly to get to know it and partly, she admitted, so she could keep a wary eye on it. The more she watched, the more she admired the snake. After an hour or so, it still hadn't moved, but Sibyl had begun to see it as a guide, rather than an enemy. She asked the snake to let her know when she should begin the hard work of wrestling with fear, and in her heart she heard it exclaim, "Go!"

To enact her ceremony of confronting fear she had chosen an area of sand and low desert plants whose boundaries she marked with a few stones. On one of the stones, representing the entrance and exit to this ceremonial ground, she sat her Teddy bear. The bear was her lifeline, the familiar, friendly object that would guide her out of the circle if, as she feared, she became so overwhelmed that she would revert back to the frightened and helpless little girl she had been. She no sooner stepped in than she immediately started screaming at her father. She screamed so loudly that I could hear her back at the base camp. Never, she told the group as she related her story, had she yelled at her father like that. Never had she told him that what he was doing was wrong. She yelled and pounded the ground with a stick and threw the red canyon dust at his imagined face. And when she was spent, she walked toward the Teddy bear, picked him up, and went back to her tarp. The snake was gone. Every day, she went into her circle at least once, sometimes twice. She castigated her father, comforted her child self, and forgave her adult self for having taken so long to confront the past. On the third day the snake returned, and she bowed before it and thanked it for guiding her. Because she had opened up to the possibility that the snake posed no danger and could, in fact, be an ally, her work on the greater fear could begin. Before she even entered that ceremonial circle for the first time, she had wrestled with a smaller, tamer angel and it had emboldened her with a blessing for her contest with the bigger angel.

Several years ago I wrote a book about the Beloved, an archetype found in many cultures. The Beloved is a divine, beguiling being who sweeps a mortal man or woman off their feet and entices them to follow the passion that calls them, no matter where it leads. In my work, the Beloved is the force in each of us that beckons us to step into arenas of life that feel at once too big for us and absolutely made for us. This seductive force could be the urge to launch a new career, to end a partnership that has long been unsatisfying, or to volunteer for an important cause. The contrasting force, the one that pulls us back as the Beloved allures us forth, is fear of not being up to the task. *Don't!* says this other force. *What if it doesn't work out? Why abandon something safe and dull for something possibly risky?* Simply by asking myself if it is fear that is bidding me not to fight the angel— or to walk into the embrace of the Beloved—I often realize that that is precisely the reason for my procrastination. That awareness gives me the impetus to move ahead.

And when I declare *Yes* to a strong and wondrous force that has tapped me, of all people, to engage with it, I revolt against apathy, fear, and powerlessness and step forth to give my life a new and higher meaning. I assert, in fact, the importance of something that could just possibly affect lives other than my own. I take on a meaning, a need, a wild horse saddled with stirrups that are just the right length for my legs. Shouting *No* to the contradictory forces that would shut me down and shut me up, I am also shouting, *Yes* to the Beloved, to my own possible future, to becoming more intimately and intricately engaged with the world. And in that moment, I realize that I need others, allies, who are also willing to shout out *Yes*. (In Sibyl's case, the snake, the Teddy bear, and the other members of the group were allies.) Now my defiance is no longer strictly personal. It has become communal. Ceasing to be silent and nursed shyly in my own heart alone, my commitment to fight the angel roars out and breaks bonds. It is free and in the freedom it grabs beauty. And so I proclaim, *NO! I will not be silenced! I will not hold back! I will not live in fear! I will love what I love. With this declaration of NO, I simultaneously declare YES to a life of meaning, beauty, and joy.*

III. SEEK

To track beauty in the depths of grief and joy in the midst of brokenness is to gain a new understanding of balance. Wonder, gratitude, a sense of belonging, delight in some ordinary moment, a brave step into a scary unknown—these jolts of grace do not replace grief. Nor do they come automatically, just because we're sad and the universe decides we deserve a break. If that were so, we would be shallower individuals, rushing through tribulation in order to get our payoff. We would assume that, once we find this balance, we will never have to look back at what we've learned from our time in the darkness. We would think our work was done. Finding balance, *maintaining* balance, requires gazing regularly into the precincts of the opposite pole with the conviction that there could be some treasure there.

13. Open up to the possibility of mystery.

Where will I get the money to pay this month's bills? Will the weather clear up, so I can take a hike today? What's going to happen to my son if he doesn't quit using cocaine? Which of the colleges I've applied to should I attend?

Some questions excite a sense of mystery. Some plague with uncertainty.

Mystery and uncertainty have a lot in common. In both states of unknowing I confront a blank canvas. Something is unresolved: an answer, a direction I can't discern eludes me. I feel like a traveler looking for a place to sleep after a long journey, wondering where I'll end up. When it's uncertainty I face, I'm urgently grasping for answers. I feel incomplete, and my incompleteness shows up as a need, a hunger, a desperation for solid ground and road signs to point me ahead. I'm twitchy and uncomfortable and desperate to get out of the deep hole of unknowing I find myself in.

When I engage with mystery, on the other hand, that sense of incompleteness tingles with a form of expectation that lacks urgency. I sense that the unknown is beckoning me ahead, rather than threatening me from behind. I'm excited about what may occur, but not impatient for it, or at least not *too* impatient. I might feel some anxiety, for I know that if I step into new and untried ground, I may be tested. And yet, if I follow the allure instead of the fear, let the glimmer of mystery shine brighter than the fog that's shrouding it, I feel excited. I know that things will emerge that I just haven't noticed before.

To open myself to the possibility of mystery, I must cultivate the kind of mindfulness that Ortega y Gassett ascribes to a skilled hunter. The hunter never knows what's going to happen next and must therefore be constantly attentive to any shift in the environment—the crack of a twig, a slight horizontal movement of brown fur amidst the gray verticality of the forest—that will mark the stealthy passage of the animal she's tracking. Attuned to the animal and acutely aware that the animal might also be attuned to her own human presence, the hunter must "create an attention that does not consist in riveting itself to the presumed but consists precisely in not presuming anything and avoiding inattentiveness."[1] In other words, the attention, fixed upon a field of possibility, will flare into action when the one right thing makes itself manifest. Before that happens, the hunter—or the confused human that any of us may be—abides in the mystery with curiosity, patience, stillness, and cunning.

In his book *Becoming Wild* Carl Safina describes a version of this patient alertness to the presence of animals that is just the opposite of stalking it in a hunt to kill. Traveling in a research boat with sperm whale researcher Shane Gero, Safina and the crew spent many hours each day watching the ocean and waiting for a whale to emerge to blow. "We stare into the dazzling chop, searching shimmering shards of brightness for evidence of breath. The boat rocks. The sea rolls. The ocean is pure glitter."[2] The team knew that the whales were in the vicinity, fully immersed in the water, perhaps as deep as a thousand yards but that, unexpectedly, at any moment, they could burst to the surface. The mystery glided below, fully formed, yet unrevealed to the eager, fascinated humans who could only wait. It's a great metaphor. We never know when some invitation into mystery could fan out into a new pathway that shapes our life—or whether it's simply the first step into a dead end. Either way, as Pema Chödrön has written, the happiest people are the ones who are comfortable with uncertainty.

Allowing mystery into my life instead of trying to make sense of things or wrangle a premature decision, I can exist in a sense of excitement rather than anxiety. Instead of struggling to find out *why something happened* to me, I discover new meaning through how I handle the mystery. I practice alertness to the appearance of clues that could guide me: a book I discover on a bookstore table that seems to shout out its title, a comment by a friend, a conversation overheard in the drugstore. A writer friend told me that she once got clear on what she needed to do with an article she was working on that had been confounding her when she heard Chef Tom Colicchio advise one of the *Top Chef* contestants to "Cook your own food!" She realized that she had been omitting from her article the exact information that was her own experiential "food" and that by incorporating it, the piece would finally be on target.

We are forced to box with mystery and uncertainty whenever we undergo a crisis. Beginning in 2020, the uncertainties of the pandemic made many of us more acutely aware of how we are going to need to adapt to the increasing challenges of climate change, which, unlike even the most virulent super-virus, is going to stretch our species for generations, not just months or years. As much as we long for the bad times to end, we can get through them a little easier if we are constantly on the lookout for the mystery in the monster. So immense, so polymorphous, so unpredictable, so relentless is climate change that it invites us to move beyond our plaintive begging for meaning in personal and local crises and begin to experiment with how we will live with, enact, and initiate new meaning. Then again, that is what every tragedy invites of us, if only we are brave enough and curious enough about the mystery to explore it.

14. Look for where the smiling ends.

I learned a lesson about human vulnerability from a grainy, seven-minute, black and white film called "Where the Smiling Ends." The film was too short to sit down for, so to see it you stood in front of a small screen embedded in a wall of Baltimore's American Museum of Visionary Art. I watched it over and over. You could tell that no one had paid any attention to Andi Olsen on that day she positioned her camera in front of Trevi Fountain in Rome. She was just one person among thousands who visited the famous landmark that day and aimed their cameras at it. Few people would have lingered long enough after having their own presence there memorialized to notice how one woman came and stayed. All around the crowded fountain the visitors found a spot where they positioned themselves singly, in pairs, in family groups, and brought up their smiles. It's what you do when you're before a camera, everyone knows that: you demonstrate your gladness to be where you are. The designated photographers aimed, focused, clicked, and the moment belonged to the posterity of albums all over the world. A certain someone had been to Trevi Fountain and here was the evidence to prove it.

The subject of Olsen's film, however, was not the smiling face of a fellow traveler in a storied place. What she was interested in was what happened to all those people right after the shutter clicked and the camera was lowered. Set to the music of Samuel Barber's "Adagio for Strings," the film shows in slow motion how one posed face after another releases the enthusiasm they have ratcheted up for the camera. At first, the vanishing of these smiles strikes the viewer as little more than a tail-end version of the "live" photos that animate a second of action before an iPhone shot. But as the video continues, something else becomes painfully evident. Olsen has offered her viewers an intimate glimpse into that instant when the essential self, like a tide rushing in to a hollow of rocks, fills the space carved out by public expectation. Husbands and wives, teenagers, lovers, grandparents, friends—one after another they stop smiling, and what replaces the smile is the person we are when we assume we're alone and unwitnessed. Over and over again the falling-off of the smile reveals each face dissolving into its own solitary and wistful world. Often the smile fades with a bow of the head, as if the effort of manufacturing that expression and keeping one's chin up has been exhausting. Each face, supposedly unobserved, retreats to a private corner of sorrow, envy, boredom, resignation, or relief. The people in Olsen's film are saying something much different from what they assumed their photos would later say. They aren't saying, "This is me in front of Trevi Fountain!" They're saying, "I stood in front of Trevi Fountain, and it has fixed absolutely nothing in my life."

When I came across this video, I felt that Andi Olsen had discovered how to see people's souls and how to reveal them to others. And when I turned around after watching it a few times, the world had transformed. It was as if I could see in every person I encountered that inner place where the smiling ends. Men, women, children, serious museum goers, bored students on a field trip—I seemed to see, without knowing the slightest detail of the life of any of them, that there was something they were worried about, something they desperately wanted, something that had happened to hurt their feelings. I fell in love with all of them. Andi Olsen reminds us of how quickly and poignantly, if we pay attention, we can glimpse the authenticity of another.

Rilke was familiar with this place of coming home to the private, vulnerable state of ourselves. In his *Notes of Malte Laurids Brigge*, he writes:

> We discover that we do not know our role; we look for a mirror; we want to remove our make-up and take off what is false and be real. But somewhere a piece of disguise that we forgot still sticks to us. A trace of exaggeration remains

in our eyebrows; we do not notice that the corners of our mouths are bent. And so we walk around, a mockery and a mere half: neither having achieved being nor actors.[1]

Olsen's film shows people as they let their disguises unstick. Watching them, we realize that, somewhere in us, too, and in our friends, our kids, the cashier in Home Depot, the hitchhiker on the highway— somewhere the smiling ends. In each person there is a public face that winks on when it has to and then, excused from the effort, fades. Paradoxically, it is when we gain compassion for the fundamental aloneness of others that our own sense of aloneness fades, for we see that the private, ineffable self is as much a part of being human as a lung or a gall bladder.

In times of hardship, it's easy to become so wound up in myself that I come to believe that no one else has problems like mine, and therefore that all attention should be riveted on me until I say otherwise. I might get annoyed if someone behaves toward me as if I'm not suffering, as if they don't see that my particular burdens are much heavier than theirs. Yet I do myself a favor if I open myself up to perceive that place in others where the public self dissolves into the private soul. If I look for where the smiling ends when I meet a refugee family who has fled their homeland and settled in a place I think of as "mine," or when I say good morning to the neighbor who annoys me because he has piled dozens of bags of garbage behind his house, or talk calmly to some anonymous person on the other end of the telephone help line when what I really want to do is scream at her after my long wait on hold—when I do that, I remember that, in each of them, there is a place where the smiling ends. As a bonus, I also get a glimpse into where the smile begins. Subtly, with little ado, I recognize that there are moments when this person's enchantment replaces loneliness, fascination unseats boredom, appreciation drives out disapproval. This person has been a smiling baby and may have smiled down at their own smiling child. They have thrown their arms around another in a burst of uncontainable love and longed desperately for that one thing that would make their lives so much better.

During the coronavirus pandemic, some people proclaimed that "we're all in this together," while others countered, "No, we are not all in this together, because if you're a white person with a nice house and a comfortable savings account, you're in a very different place from a poor person of color who's lost their job." Both statements are true. The trouble with each is that, if we hold tight to either as the single right opinion, we miss the other part of the equation. If we only assume we're all in it together, we overlook the many who are suffering. If we only believe that some hold more of a title to suffering than others, then we dismiss or even disparage a lot of real pain. We are all suffering from fear; many, regardless of income, are suffering from grief over the death of a loved one; and many millions are suffering from financial insecurity. The reality that we are all mourning something is the great and terrible shadow of this virus, and it is the even bigger and more lasting shadow of the climate crisis. COVID-19 infected millions of people; the radical warming of Planet Earth will affect billions, and no mask or observance of social distancing will protect us. We will survive better if we remember that all people harbor within their being a place where the smiling ends and where it begins.

15. Bear responsibility. Don't collapse under it.

It was their family custom. Whenever Victoria Markham returned home, her two young sons, aged seven and three and a half, would rush out to greet her. On this particular day, Victoria didn't notice when the youngest, Koa, slipped behind the car. As she was maneuvering into her parking spot, the car bumped his leg. The little boy fell and hit his head on a stone wall. Hours later he died.

How does one live with such horror? Compounding the grief is the knowledge that your actions, the exact way you steered that car for two or three seconds, led to a loss you will never recover from. Grief tears us apart. Responsibility, regret, and grief burn our very core. Any one of them is agonizing. Imagine them all together, pummeling you every day. You were responsible for a terrible thing. You cannot escape that truth. And the other truth is that your grief is bottomless, for there is nothing in the world that you can do to fix this thing. So what will you do about it?

That awful blend of grief and responsibility roil in all of us who feel the burgeoning horror of the climate crisis.

Here is a list whose contents you're probably at least somewhat familiar with. It's from a 2017 report by the Union of Concerned Scientists, identifying real physical signs that global warming is no longer a phenomenon to be staved off, but rather a clear and immediate danger. As you read these facts, pay attention to your emotional reaction.

1. Arctic sea ice extent is diminishing: Areas of the Earth covered by sea ice are shrinking by an average of 3.2 percent per year.

2. Ocean heat content is increasing: As the top half-mile of the oceans warms, coral reefs die, marine ecosystems collapse, and global fisheries cease to function.

3. Air temperature over the oceans is increasing: Warmer air near the surface of the ocean leads to increased evaporation, causing more water vapor, which may contribute to more violent hurricanes.

4. Global sea level is rising: As the waters get higher, millions of coastal homelands around the world are flooded, freshwater is contaminated, and homelessness, disease, and death impact vast populations.

5. Air temperature over land is increasing faster than over the oceans: This means that insect pests proliferate, challenging plants, animals, and humans.

6. Snow cover is reduced, and snow is melting faster: Rising temperatures mean that less snow falls in the Northern Hemisphere, and snowpacks are melting earlier. Millions of people around the world rely on melting snow to replenish their water supplies, and this shift threatens existence.[1]

How did you feel as you read this dire information? Did you skim each item, telling yourself you already know this stuff and don't need to read it again? Did you pause occasionally to absorb the data, so you'd understand the science a little better? Did you feel an ache in your gut that worsened as you moved from one number to the next? It's easy to read each statistic, experience a rise of unpleasant emotion, and then try to detour around the feeling by moving on to the next item in the list. But when you allow the information to sink in, not just to your consciousness but also to your heart, how can you feel anything but sadness and horror and probably guilt as well? These six points and four others in the report that aren't included here are not scenarios for a science fiction movie, they are forecasts, as sure as December ascends on the tail of November.

I am not going to expound here on all the data proving that humans are causing this crisis. If you're reading this book, you are all too aware of that. I present this list not to make you feel bad, but to remind you that *feeling bad because you had a hand in what's happening is appropriate.* The question is, *How do we take responsibility for the state of the planet without collapsing under the weight of powerlessness, regret, guilt, and shame?* It's the same question Victoria Markham had to ask herself after the death of her child: *How do I go on when I know I have been the cause of something so unspeakably awful?* Acceptance of responsibility, guilt, and shame are three ways of existing with the knowledge that we have been the cause of a terrible event. Are they all important states of being that we should be learning how to bear?

White middle-class Baby Boomers like me and those of the generations that immediately preceded and followed mine—ordinary people, not oil tycoons—know that we hold some responsibility for the collapse of natural systems on Earth because of actions we have taken over the years. When were growing up, we took those actions in innocence. We thought it was fine, and indeed socially expected, to buy a new car every few years, to fly to some enticing new place for vacation, and then, as internet technology became the shopping mall of the century, to sit in our own homes and select from an infinite supply of enticing new books and smart phones, computers and boots that would be flown to our homes from all over the world. Now, when we—when *I*—take these actions, I can no longer delude myself that I am innocent. I act in full knowledge that my actions are harmful, and yet I continue to drive and fly and buy anyway. As a direct result of my actions, the Earth and all her people bear a heavy burden. Yes, yes, I am not as guilty as the decision-makers and fossil fuel perpetrators at Exxon, Saudi Aramco, or United Airlines. But I am nevertheless responsible for raising the temperature of my beautiful home planet and contributing to a frightening future for all living beings.

Surveys show that every generation, from Baby Boomers to Gen Z, suffers more anxiety about climate change than the generation before. "Why should I want to live in this world that doesn't care?" asked one youth in response to a study that the global nonprofit Avaaz sponsored to determine how children and youth are dealing with climate change. As this heartbreaking cry proves, the short answer to the survey's focus is, *They are in despair.* They blame their governments for not doing more. They can't understand how their parents and grandparents could have been so neglectful of the future of their descendants. The study showed that nearly half the youth surveyed in ten countries feel so much anxiety about global warming that it affects their sleeping, eating, and studying habits. Seventy-five percent viewed the future as "frightening."[2] Young people bear less responsibility for the problem and far more consequences. But it is nonetheless true that every single one of us must live with the knowledge that our plane flights, our aimless and amiable Saturday night drives around town with friends, our upgraded cell phone and the one after that and the one after that, and the hamburgers we grilled that came from cows munching grass in a Brazilian pasture that used to be a rainforest—that each of these little pleasures has added to the sickness of the Earth.

Some environmentalists think that feeling guilt or even shame for our actions is good for us, that it serves as a preventative measure against doing even more harm. Guilt is different from shame, as William L. Jordan points out in his book, *The Sunflower Forest*. Shame, unlike guilt, "is not the response of the conscience to what we *do*, but of our consciousness of what we *are*.... Shame, in this sense— what I call existential shame—may arise from a wrongdoing, but it is not associated only with moral failure. It is rather a sense of existential unworthiness."[3] Shame is the clinging monster that Sibyl was determined to deal with when she set off into a Utah canyon to confront the sexual abuse her father had inflicted on her. Shame is toxic. You're ashamed when you're implicated in some action that you don't want anyone to know about, because if they do, they'll know you to be filthy and despicable. Personally, I would not recommend shame as an ecological motivator.

The Swedes are so committed to the appropriateness of feeling badly about climate change that they coined a word, *Flygskam*, for one aspect of it. Flight-shame is the unease you feel when you book a flight, even though you are fully aware of the amount of carbon it will release into the atmosphere. When Greta Thunberg, Sweden's most celebrated advocate of climate shame, traveled to the United

States in 2016, she took a solar-powered yacht. Some people made fun of her, perhaps because her action reminded them and all of us of what we ourselves were *not* doing to reduce carbon emissions.

A little guilt isn't so bad. If I take an unwise action, like buying a bag of California avocados each week at my New York supermarket, I may feel guilt. I will have to admit that I have made avocados more important than the health of the Earth. But if I keep on taking those guilty actions that I know to be harmful (weekly avocados, new smartphone), the guilt may burn hotter and hotter until it becomes shame. Then shame makes me feel as if I am being observed and harshly judged. Eventually, perhaps, this knot of emotions may pain me enough so I stop behaving in that way.

Moreover, if those of us who are white descendants of colonial settlers are honest with ourselves, we must take on other heavy responsibilities. We live where we do, at our own home address, with our lawn and garden, our kitchen and bedroom, our view of the sunset and resident birds, because our ancestors stole the land from indigenous people. Or, even if they themselves didn't steal it, they have been trading in it ever since. And even if we white people aren't the grandchildren and great-grandchildren of slaveowners, we must nevertheless bear the responsibility of white privilege that has marked our assumptions, fostered since we were born, about how we get to lead our lives when others don't have the same advantages because they were not born Caucasian. If we try to escape these burdens, it's only our awareness of it that we temporarily manage to slough off, as if we've taken a painkiller or slipped a blindfold over our eyes. But no matter how numb and momentarily distracted we are, the burden itself remains on our shoulders and won't be shaken off.

The recognition of our responsibility for the state of the world we live in is a burden we have to live with. How, then, will we do it? If you carry a backpack up to the top of a mountain, you take up a destination, a project, a physical weight, and a spiritual goal all in one. Once I did a forty-one-mile solo hike on the Resurrection Pass

Trail on Alaska's Kenai Peninsula. I was an experienced backpacker, but during those five days of elevation, mosquitoes, rain, and isolation, I sometimes wondered why I had decided that such an arduous task would be a good idea. The pack was heavy. I was fifty-three years old. I got a big blister on my heel, and I worried about grizzly bears. Yet I could not, would not have wanted to stop. I had launched this project, I had gathered the necessary supplies and organized them in my pack, and I was carrying my world on my back. There had been a beginning to the journey, and there would be an end, and I wanted to get there to that end, with my gear and on my own feet. And anyway, all around me, every minute was such wild beauty. When I made it to the end of the trail, I was exhilarated and very proud of myself.

Can we bear the burden of climate change and be proud of our acceptance of the challenge, the responsibility? Pride, as it turns out, may be a bigger motivator of ecologically responsible behavior than guilt or shame, according to a study by Princeton University.[4] Researchers asked 987 people to write an essay expressing either pride or guilt about the action they would take in a specific environmental scenario. Those who imagined being proud of themselves were more inclined to take the "right" action than those who would have felt shame. It's much nicer to feel good about something you've done than to feel bad. Shame makes you want to hide. And since bearing the responsibility of the demise of Earth as we know it is the backpack we all have to carry now, it will behoove us to do it with love and compassion and a fierce consciousness of the beauty that is (still) all around us. There is nothing I can do to reverse what happened, but there is much I can do to live differently in the present and have it count in the future.

Victoria Markham was crushed by grief over the loss of her son, a grief compounded by the responsibility she felt because she had inadvertently caused his death. Over time she developed several ways to live with these painful feelings by confronting them in herself and helping others to do so. Before the accident, she was already a life coach; afterwards she became a grief counselor and began working with other people in grief to help them live with their loss. She spoke at length with Native Americans in her area, for she realized that in their cultures, grief is an inevitability handled with friendship and ceremony, rather than in isolation, and she wanted to understand how that kind of mutual support could be fostered in a non-indigenous community. She also created a workshop in which the participants, all of whom were grieving a loss, created something beautiful out of what was broken. First, everyone spent several hours making a ceramic pot, which they glazed, and fired. Then they deliberately broke this beautiful thing. What had been was no more. Everyone held the broken pieces in their hands and experienced grief over the loss of the pot and, in a much greater sense, all that was irreparably broken in their life and that had brought them to the workshop. Then they undertook the repair. They filled the cracks of the pot with gold, remembering in the process that, although that which is broken can never be made whole again, we do have the ability to give it a whole new kind of beauty.

16. Imagine the end of the world—but not the end of the story.

For as long as I can remember, I have been driven to plot my survival through calamity. When I was a little girl and my mother went out for the evening, I insisted on knowing exactly when she'd be back. If she said, for example, nine o'clock, and she wasn't home by one minute past, my body, like a time bomb, exploded with fear. I would stand at the big picture window in the dark dining room, staring out at the street in anticipation of the one pair of headlights that would slow, then make their perfect, palliative swerve into our driveway. As the seconds dragged past, the fear grew and my imagination got to work: What would I do if my mother didn't come home? Who would I call to help me find out what had happened to her? Who would take care of my little brother and me? How would I get to school? My father must have been in the lamplit living room just on the other side of the entry hall, his open briefcase, his papers from work, and his bottle of gin at hand, but it never occurred to me either to go to him for help or to consider him among the emergency actions I might have to resort to.

There are two kinds of selves in every human being, wrote Robert Jay Lifton in his book about the effects of the atomic bomb on the people of Hiroshima. The interviews he conducted with survivors, *hibakusha*, of the blast led him to distinguish between the "measured self," which is concerned with ordinary life in ordinary time, and the "apocalyptic self," which vaults into the fray when life as we know it is under immediate threat. We need both selves, Lifton writes. "We need the ordinary self to remember that life in its simple living is of value, and we need the apocalyptic self for its awareness of potential catastrophe.... Hiroshima was an 'end of the world, and yet the world still exists."[1]

Similarly, Michael Ortiz Hill points out that all of us are sustained by certain vital phenomena, those elements of "simple living" we take for granted—and, indeed, need to take for granted to a certain extent in order to make the countless decisions that are required of us every day. When something happens to undermine the sense of safety and well-being that we count on deriving from these ordinary and reassuring forces—warm bed at night, first cup of coffee in the morning, putting your contact lenses in and seeing the world anew—we feel raw, exposed, endangered, and frightened. The first two decades of the twenty-first century have triggered the apocalyptic self in ways that many of us alive today never imagined we would have to experience. The COVID-19 pandemic, as well as the catastrophic hurricanes, floods, tornadoes, and wildfires that swept over the planet, and for Americans, the lies, violence, and hatred that bled the 2020 presidential election and its aftermath, forced us to acknowledge the end of the world as we had known it. That harsh awakening compelled us to imagine a still more apocalyptic reality: a world where new plagues strike relentlessly and little remains of a scorching planet but the waste products of plastic and plutonium. How would we survive? How would we find enough meaning, beauty, and compassion to nourish us, even assuming we could garner the shelter, food, income, and health care we would need to keep ourselves and our loved ones going?

"Western philosophy has long realized that we must imagine our own death in order to live more fully," Lifton writes. "After Hiroshima, however, our further task is to imagine the end of the world in order to take steps to maintain human existence." [2] Imagining the end of the world is not the same as imagining the end of the story. What I was doing as a little girl, standing at the window and worrying that my mother might not come back home, was imagining the end of the story. Incapable at that age of plotting solutions, I was just tumbled about by fearful questions. Lifton says that imagining the end of the world does not specifically mean the end of my or any one person's individual world; it's the end of the shared, collective life of the wider community that we have to take into consideration. In 1945 and the years following the war, the

77

community that had ended for many Japanese was Hiroshima. In the twenty-first century the community whose ending we anticipate is the whole planet.

The one thing we absolutely must do after the end of the world is create a new world. That is the enormous burden of all of us today, and it will be more of a burden for every coming generation. As young people look to the future, they see how the normal anxieties that people of their age used to feel about what the future might bring are now weighted with the knowledge that their entire planet is in the early stages of collapse. Nuclear war was a fearsome possibility when I was growing up. Climate change is a certainty. Just a few months before the coronavirus pandemic struck, my stepson told me that his two sons, who were then in their first and fourth years of college, had three grave concerns: (1) climate change, (2) getting shot in their classroom, and (3) not being able to find a job after they graduated. Then came COVID, when the consolations of home, college, friendships, and social life that they depended on to maintain their senses of humor and sanity cracked apart. Young people know that what probably awaits their adulthood is mental and physical hardship, mass migration, vanishing species, and an even more worrisome future for their own children if they dare to have them. There is no safety net. We are, we will be in constant danger and unable to relax

Forced to battle such an amorphous, invisible enemy, the collective mind, not surprisingly, conjures up a more recognizable, and perhaps more vulnerable, stand-in. Zombies and vampires have been haunting the living since medieval times, reports Jason Zinoman in the *New York Times*. Back then, when people didn't know that sickness spread from one person to another, they attributed plague and pestilence to monstrous creatures who roamed through the towns and infected "every house with disease and death with... pestiferous breath."[3] These half-human, half-alive beings continue to feature prominently in dystopian literature, music, art, and film popular today. They make perfect scapegoats, for they are alien enough to do a lot of damage in ways that are hard to understand and harder to control, yet their close resemblance to humans convinces the terrified populace that they can eventually be conquered and even befriended.

Other variations on the end-of-life-as-we-know-it story depict scenarios of a scorched, dead, planet where only the scrappiest and cleverest are able to survive. Many youth find refuge in this kind of media, explains Laurence Steinberg, a psychologist at Temple University, because it reflects, magnifies, and clarifies their own preoccupations. "Their brains are very responsive to emotionally arousing stimuli. When teenagers feel sad, what they often do is put themselves in situations where they feel even sadder. So they listen to sad songs, watch sad movies."[4] Dystopian media not only mirrors their personal feelings, but also encourages them to believe that, even in the worst of times, pathways to survival are possible and they themselves might be the ones to blaze them. Identifying with characters who have special superpowers that enable them to make a positive contribution in a broken world encourages readers or movie goers to imagine what their own superpower might be and how they might one day use it to outlast the crisis and help their family and friends. In his most recent book, *The Climate Swerve*, written when he was ninety years old, Lifton emphasizes the importance of seeing ourselves as survivors as we contemplate the certain emergencies of global warming. "To avoid actual catastrophe requires that ever-increasing numbers of us take on that sense of being prospective survivors. As prospective survivors we can find meaning in our actions to combat climate change."[5]

When we imagine the end of the world, we must dare to ask ourselves, *All right then, and what next?* James Stockdale, best known for being Ross Perot's vice-presidential candidate in 1992 and stammering miserably through his televised debate with Senator Al Gore and Vice President Dan Quayle, was, in fact, a war hero. As badly as he did before a television audience of millions, he had been a power of example during the eight years that he was held captive and tortured as a prisoner of war in Vietnam. His ability to stay alive and keep his sanity during his long internment stemmed from his ability to imagine a new story. "I never lost faith in the end of the story," Stockdale, later a research fellow studying Stoic philosophy at the Hoover Institute, told author Jim Collins. "I never doubted not only that I would get out, but also that I would prevail in the end and turn the event into the defining event of my life."

Who didn't make it out? asked Collins, who was writing a book about why some people succeed, while others don't. "The optimists," Stockdale replied. "Oh, they were the ones who said, 'We're going to be out by Christmas.' And Christmas would come, and Christmas would go. Then they'd say, 'We're going to be out by Easter.' And Easter would come, and Easter would go. And then Thanksgiving, and then it would be Christmas again. And they died of a broken heart." Then Stockdale offered this advice to Collins: "You must never confuse faith that you will prevail in the end— which you can never afford to lose—with the discipline to confront the most brutal facts of your current reality, whatever they might be."[6]

It's hard to get beyond imagining the end of the world. If the world ends, I can't help asking myself, won't I end, too? Assuming I do somehow survive, if the world is gone, any direction I turn in will be unfamiliar. What tools can I possibly pick up when all the tools have been destroyed? And how can I prepare? These are ruminations that only a willingness to open to the mystery of the moment will allow. For even in the midst of the nightmare there is a next step, albeit something as apparently passive as refusing to count on the salvation of Christmas. We can more bravely imagine the end of the world if we imagine that, even then, we will have choices. We will make friends. We will fall in love. We will be required to make meals and find a place to wash. And we will be forced to expend our ingenuity in ways we have no way of predicting. It will be increasingly important in trying times for us to get together with others, to confront the reality of collapse and to boldly assert our own capacity, our own gifts for surviving and even triumphing through that future. If I only imagine the end of the world, I sink into powerlessness and despair. If I only imagine the new story, I have no solid grounding out of which to begin plotting my steps. But if I imagine the end of the world and also imagine the beginning of the story, I can get through just about anything.

17. Explore what you think you already know.

In the documentary film *Living in the Time of Dying*, Cherokee Stan Rushworth, who is also an honorary member of the Chiricahua Apache Nation, tells a story about how he learned to be present in the world. One day when he was about six years old, his grandfather, who raised him, took him to a pond and indicated with a glance that they should sit there together. The minutes passed, and the minutes passed, and the boy kept wondering what they were going to do, when the point of this adventure was going to start. With his eyes, the grandfather let him know that he should just keep sitting. Eventually, says Rushworth:

> All this life came around us, this incredibly beautiful life.....
> The frogs come up, the birds are all around us, and there are
> hundreds and hundreds and hundreds of dragonflies flying
> all around us, brilliant turquoise, really bright, intense
> crimson. Some of them are really small. Damselflies and
> others are like five inches long... and pretty soon I realized
> that the whole time they're copulating, and they're flying
> right up to me with the male or the female looking into my
> eyes and the other one attached, facing in the other direction.
> I'm six and all this life around me is having sex, and the
> energy is over the top beautiful, and I couldn't think
> anymore, I could only be there, and I could only realize I was
> completely immersed in, swallowed up in this incredible
> thing that people call nature. I looked at my grandfather, and
> he nodded.[1]

Rushworth said he later realized that this was his first ceremony.

Everything, inside of us and out, is constantly rising and falling away. This is the great lesson of Buddhism. Nothing is permanent, including those forms and concepts that seem most eternal. All the cells in your body are aging and reforming, the wood in the trees and in the window sills of your house is slowly rotting. Insect larvae and flower bulbs are swelling in the soil beneath your feet. Ideas, governments, and nations are emerging, as are the people who lead them and speak with such authority, as if they had the everlasting clue to all righteousness. And then they are all extinguished by new ideas, governments, and nations. Even our fourteen-billion-year-old universe is changing. Nothing illustrates that old truism better than the beautiful and breathtaking images sent back to Earth from the James Webb Space Telescope in the summer of 2022. They reveal a cosmos in constant motion—expanding, burning up, gobbling, spiraling, birthing.

The ephemeral nature of all things is nowhere more evident than if I sit outside, as Stan Rushworth's grandfather taught him to do, and simply pay attention. I don't need a vast wilderness area to do this practice. It works anywhere—in my backyard, in a city park, or when I stand on the bustling corner of a big city. Even there, after I settle down for a few moments and become attuned, I become witness to the Earth being itself: the light of the sky as it streams over the windows of the skyscrapers, the pigeons fluttering around dropped crumbs and then flapping away in careless synchrony, the people passing by, one after another, each intent on some private purpose. No matter where I am, light, sound, and movement sweep over me, briefly involving me in their passage, but continuing on without any need whatsoever for my participation, or even my observation. Each is itself, and each is connected with infinite others. A pigeon is itself. The one leaf on the twig that swirls, while all the others remain still, is itself. Even the windows of the skyscraper are themselves, buttressing the sky outside and people and their business within. The awareness of these passages that grows from out of my silence and attention is peaceful and soothing, and I come to realize that even my life is passing, moment by moment, year by year, until I will be no more. And that, too, is soothing.

When I talk about exploring what you think you already know, I don't mean doing research on a subject you'd like to know more about. I'm not talking about shoveling new data into the brain, but rather about absorbing what's around you when you think you've already absorbed as much as you have to. After a few minutes of this exercise of attentiveness, there will no doubt be a part of you that claps its hands together and states, *Okay, I've got the point, now let's move on!* Instead of moving on, you nestle back down for a little bit longer, a little more noticing. The early twentieth-century writer Francis Ponge advises us to let the world "disarrange" us, so that we can get to know it better. A tea kettle, a frog, a spiderweb—let it grab hold of you and tell you something vital and astonishing that you never knew before! This is a practice of opening up to the familiar. Even, perhaps especially, in the midst of hard times, we need to open up to disarrangement from our places, our friends, our objects, and the strangers who are suffering as we are or doing their best to help. A woman camped out with her family in a school gymnasium after wildfires forced them out of their California home makes it a point to ask others in that cramped, frightening, and often exceedingly dull situation what it is that gives them strength. "God," says one. "My grandchildren," says another. "I just got picked for the school gymnastics team," says another, "and I don't want to miss out when we start practicing." Their responses often inspire her, and they remind the other person that they have something valuable to share and, in fact, to live for. Together both of them are brought together in a moment of enlightenment and friendship.

Being disarranged by the world doesn't always lead to beauty and happiness. Sometimes it leads to a shocking awareness. In *Being Ecological* Timothy Morton points out that, when you think about it, ordinary things like plastic bags and Styrofoam cups are a lot more devious than we had assumed. "A plastic bag isn't just for humans. It's for seagulls to choke on…. A Styrofoam cup isn't just for coffee, it's for slowly being digested by soil bacteria for five hundred years."[2] Once I take in this disturbing awareness, I can't pick up one of those ubiquitous cups or accept a plastic bag from a shop without seeing them in an entirely new way. My awareness of Styrofoam cups and plastic bags has expanded; I recognize that they are not the small and useful items I once thought they were, but killers.

To maintain equilibrium in hard times it is imperative to open up to being surprised. Yet it is so easy now to escape boredom! If young Stan Rushworth had been born a few decades later, he might have brought his smart phone to the pond and sneaked peeks at it when his grandfather appeared not to be paying attention (he was probably always paying attention). Your phone can whisk you away from your mundane surroundings and give you access to a bright and lively non-stop world: updates on friends, gossip from colleagues, dope things to buy, new tunes. What's on your phone is not the world, however, it is a shadow world contained in a tiny rectangle that you hold in your hand. The real world is more than two feet away from your eyes, it has three dimensions, and you can step into it at any time. Its variations and shifts are slow, but they're amazing. For instance, dragonflies might stare at you.

Standing in line at the unemployment office is tedious and often debasing, but even there something or someone has the capacity to startle you. The comings and goings outside your window, or even outside the door of your hospital room, tell stories. They speak of all those who live alongside you, they offer clues, they look different from how you remembered. They have lives. There is the possibility for amazement even in chaos and turmoil, when surviving is paramount and you know that the home you left the day before may not even be there when you return. When the waters of New Orleans flooded and the levees started rushing under the front door of their home, Delores Ossevaito and her husband only had time to rescue their two dogs before dashing outside, unmooring their boat, and jumping in. For four days and nights, as the filthy waters rose and fell around them, flooding familiar neighborhoods and streets, they had nothing to eat or drink, and the boat became their home. It was tough, Ossevaito told a reporter, adding then, "It was fun sleeping in the boat, though, because we could look out and look at all the stars."[3]

18. Be on the lookout for your next teacher.

In a subway station in New York City during morning rush hour I watched as a disheveled, dirty man, who had been leaning against the wall, sank slowly to the floor. I noticed, but I did not move from my spot on the platform, where I was positioned to push quickly into the train. What did I assume about this man? That he was drunk? Homeless? Unwell? That the condition he was now in, while not exactly normal, could not possibly be a real emergency? The other people on the platform responded as I did, which is to say they did not respond at all. One young woman in that crowd of commuters, however, perhaps on her way to college or her first job, walked briskly to the man. She bent over him, touched his shoulder, spoke to him. There was nothing—not sickness, fear, dirt, embarrassment, or a time schedule—that she would permit to separate her from what she was called to do in that moment. The train arrived, and I got on, so I never witnessed how it all worked out. All I know is that that young woman stayed behind, attending to someone who needed help. Around these two souls radiated the glow of mercy.

I never forgot that woman. Her unaffected kindness changed the way I reacted to somebody else's trouble. I don't claim that I always stop to help, but I do always stanch my inclination to hurry on, as if I haven't noticed anything amiss. I consider whether I could or should pause and get somewhat involved. That young woman, minister of care to a needy other, became one of my teachers. The world is full of them if we just pay attention. They aren't the teachers we have in school, the ones who are assigned to us by the institutional purveyors of such things, the ones who stand before us expounding on the subjects they want us to master. They're not even the spiritual teachers we are drawn to because they embody an approach to existence or God that we aspire to. The kinds of teachers I'm talking about are the ones who enter our life unexpectedly and stay just long enough to impart exactly what it is we most need to know at that time. When I witnessed an act of kindness in a subway station, I was not aware that I needed to learn that particular lesson. If I had been able to order a lesson from a menu, it probably would have been something quite different, like a great idea for a project I was struggling to conceive. But that was the one that presented itself, and gratefully I accepted the offer.

How do I attune myself to the teachers who pass by in all directions, going about their business, doing what they do just because they are themselves? The world around me swirls with intentions, and most of them have nothing to do with me. But every now and then, one of those intentions-en-route bumps right into me, as surely as if it was driven by a guide determined to alert me of something I absolutely need to know. These teachers can be friends or colleagues, strangers or even characters in a book or TV show. As for the message bearers themselves, they rarely seek me out deliberately with a view toward imparting their wisdom in blunt language. No, they and their lessons are more subtle, conveyed through action, a response to the moment, like helping a stranger in need when everyone else is intent on cramming into the subway at rush hour. I think of these teachers, often anonymous, as belonging to the class of "voiceless" ones described by Vi tagʷ-sablu Hilbert, an elder and storyteller of the Upper Skagit tribes of the Salish Nation. In an interview in *Parabola* Magazine, she explained that there is no word for "teacher" in her native language, Lushootseed: "The closest is *dasu gusage* (*ugʷusaȥ*)," she said, "someone who gives you important information. The wise things that he or she gives to you are *Kwadhakk: (xʷdikʷ)*: instruction, important information, and teachings. The word can also be translated as 'voiceless blowing sound.' So much of the important information is voiceless. It comes to you not in words of instruction but as signals: 'This is right. This is not okay.' "[1]

The natural world is a great teacher. Nature doesn't preach about the future, doesn't give you a road map for the next phase of your life or even the next hour of your day. Nature speaks strictly in the present tense. When trees and rivers and crabgrass speak, they do so as that "voiceless blowing sound" Hilbert speaks of. Yet their singular communiques have the power to strike you with the force and intensity of a piercing statement aimed right at you. A young man named James joined one of the twelve-day wilderness programs I was co-guiding, because he and his wife were expecting their first baby, and he wanted guidance on how to be a good father. His own father had been remote and punitive and, although James wanted to behave much differently with his child, he felt he didn't know how. The spot he chose for his three-day solo was in the midst of a forest of tall spruce trees. When he had first encountered them, he had been awed by their majesty, and he figured they'd be good role models to teach him about parenting.

By the middle of the third day, however, the big trees had revealed nothing, and James was worried. The following morning, he would be returning to base camp, so he didn't have much time left to get his teaching. He decided to speak aloud to the forest and tell it what he was longing for. As he was did so, something swam into to his attention that he had completely overlooked for two and a half days. Growing up beneath the old trees were dozens of young seedlings. James got up and went to explore them. He admired their soft needles, their pliable boughs, and was moved by how vulnerable they seemed. All his attention veered now toward the young trees. He went to his backpack and dug out the wooden flute he had brought along. Then he walked slowly among the seedlings, playing his flute for them and stroking each one on its feathery boughs. When he returned to base camp the following day and told his story, he was joyful, because his interaction with the young trees had taught him that his own innate qualities of tenderness and caring were the very ones he could and would bring to fatherhood.

Great teachers can emerge anywhere. The video game *Endling*, introduced in 2021, casts players in the role of a mother fox living in an apocalyptic world. She and her three kits have managed to survive the cataclysm, but food is scarce, many dangers lurk, and a curious, playful young fox can easily get into trouble. When you play the game, you have to use your senses of smell, hearing, and keen eyesight to survive in this broken and burning habitat. You have to teach the young ones important skills, like how to free themselves from a trap, search a pile of garbage for food, and scramble up a tree for safety. Instead of taking on the persona of a macho superhero with an endless armory of weapons, as in so many video games, in *Endling* you are a female animal trying to stay alive and protect those in your care.

Sometimes we reach a stage of life when we feel spiritually bankrupt or purposeless, and we begin actively seeking a teacher whose guidance we hope will set us on the right path. If we succeed in finding such a guide, we may follow them on a long, difficult, and often profound journey, as author-disciples like Irina Tweedie and Peter Matthiessen have documented in their books. If we're not so fortunate, we may discover that we have attached ourselves to a guru who abuses his wisdom and charisma by taking advantage of his students sexually or amassing wealth and luxury for himself. Whether or not we become a disciple of a spiritual teacher, we can still, and always, be on the lookout for the ephemeral teachers of the world. They wait for us in all kinds of places, like subways and forests, and their messages, imparted in just moments, can inform the rest of our lives.

To absorb these messages, we have to cultivate a sense of openness, receptivity, and restful curiosity. Unlike the fox kits in the *Endling* game, eager to play with or taste any new and interesting gobbet of their world, the curiosity entailed in seeking teachers is more discerning. We note what has heart and meaning just for us. We feel some dry bundle of kindling deep in our psyche suddenly beginning to crackle with a spark of fire. We feel moved, enticed. Our consciousness jolts. Yet if we're not careful, we can be led astray even by the impromptu prophets of life. If we try to torque a message into a form that suits what we want, rather than what we really need to know, we will overlook the real teachers and dig ourselves into selfishness. If I'm in the supermarket and I see somebody surreptitiously taking a steak out of the case and sliding it into his coat pocket, I will be wise not to consider attempting the same thing myself. The teachings I take in must feel not only right, incisive, and personal, but ethical and fair as well. They must have a deep validity, a resonance within me that is bigger than the moment and has an impact that will influence me from that time forth and in many aspects of my life. A message that makes an impression on me may very well mean nothing to you. In fact, you probably won't even notice it.

In hard times, it's easy to become so bound in my own struggles that I forget to keep an eye out for my next teacher. I may even reject a possible teacher and their counsel, judging it as irrelevant. But if I'm open, I discover that marvelous lessons abound. In the story I related about Courtney Miles, the young man who inspired his friends to commandeer New Orleans buses and rescue people stranded by Hurricane Katrina, there is another inspiring figure who barely got any notice. This was the stranger in the shelter who gave Miles a credit card, so he could buy more gas and drive through the storm back to New Orleans to pick up more people. That person was homeless and desperate too and yet, seeing a need and responding, he or she offered generosity out of an extraordinary sense of trust. Who among the crowd in that shelter packed with worried people noticed this act of kindness and was moved by it? We don't even know the name of that person or their age or gender. But the gesture reaches out from the story and grabs those who need to be grabbed by it.

IV. RECEIVE

In the bleakest of circumstances a shaft of wonder or relief can suddenly jolt you. It is entirely appropriate to grasp this gift and hold onto it. I'm not advising a forced shift in outlook: *Look on the bright side! Think positive! Be happy!* I mean that, during those times of sorrow and stress, we can lean into the beauty side of the balance and receive it fully, receive it without restraint. We allow ourselves to be enlightened, moved, soothed. We can imagine the new story, welcome the dolphins, seek that place where the smiling stops—and know that this reopening into life's promise is neither an aberration nor a cure for the sorrow it briefly comforts. The more we open to the possibility of light, the more the light will find its way in.

19. Hold the feathers of grief and joy.

In October 2010, six months after BP's Deep Water Horizon rig exploded and began spewing oil into the Gulf of Mexico, and three months after the well had been capped, Radical Joy for Hard Times organized an event called Gulf Coast Rising. We invited people living in coastal areas hit by the oil spill to spend a day giving beauty and generosity to friends and to the land, water, and animals of the Gulf. The offerings were diverse and personal. In Alabama a group of friends gathered for dinner and storytelling. At the annual Voodoo Festival in New Orleans, the renowned Treme Brass Band, wearing Gulf Coast Rising t-shirts, dedicated a song to the people's resilience and entreated the audience to raise their arms aloft in solidarity. In Florida a woman did a ceremony for endangered oysters. For our event my collaborator on the project, Margaret Saizan, and I drove from her home in Baton Route to Grand Isle, where we joined some of her friends. The southern shore of this long, pencil-shaped island just south of the Louisiana mainland faces the open water of the Gulf, so it was directly in line of the surge of oil and the chemical dispersants dumped into the water to break the oil up. The fishing businesses of families on the island had been decimated, and vast numbers of wildlife had died from the oil that greased their feathers, clogged their digestive tracts, and spurted through their blowholes.

But on that autumn morning, to an eye unhindered by the brain's knowledge of what had occurred, everything looked beautiful. The sun was shining and the water was midnight blue. Before us, over the seawall, the Gulf gave no indication that for weeks a full-scale emergency had rolled in, although in the bayous off to the west we could see enormous clawed vehicles getting on with the beach clean-up. We turned inland and began our project. Over the years Margaret and her friends had created several labyrinths in public places, and our plan was to make a large one here in the sand and fill it with birdseed as a gift for the wildlife.

We were just finishing when we noticed that a pod of dolphins had swum up no more than fifteen feet from the seawall. We hopped out of the labyrinth and dashed over to watch. The dolphins dove and rose, dove and rose, stitching together water and air with those arcing leaps known as "porpoising." Our first, shared reaction was utter delight. Those dolphins seemed nothing less than a visitation, a gift, a token of life and possibility at a dark time. For a few minutes we stood together on the wall exulting as we watched them. Soon, though, a cloud of foreboding began to slip over us as we realized that every time the dolphins quit the clear blue air and rejoined the water, they were returning to a lethal habitat. Although the well had been capped, the Gulf was still toxic. The dolphins were at the top of the food chain, and that chain of nourishment was poisoned all the way down the line. We fell silent. These animals could not possibly survive long. They were playful and exuberant and right before us, and they were likely doomed. It was difficult to balance that dual knowing, but it was the only possible response to the moment. All we could do was stand on this fragile, frightening edge, taking in the worst and the best in one moment. Neither the joy nor the sorrow would have been as acute without the presence of the other.

Longer than I have known almost anything else, I have known this: that I can survive only by holding gently, like a feather in each palm, the anguish and the beauty of being alive. My own back yard taught me this when I was very young. Until my parents divorced, my back yard was more than a place to play. It was a sanctuary, and it was my primary teacher about staying available to reality in all its varieties. In my yard I learned two lessons about surviving that I took to heart: first, that nature does not lie, and second, that it has room for everything: life, death, mutation, disintegration, blooming, hatching, fighting. Everything. It deals with what it's got. When I stepped out the back door on days after my father's drunken rages, I felt bruised and overexposed. I felt decades older than my little brother, older, even, than my mother, whom I had to watch out for, since she was the target of my father's violence and because she innocently believed his promises. I was convinced that my task was to bear the real knowledge about our precarious situation. I lived with dread of the next outburst in my father's cycle of rage and regret, rage and regret, but I also believed that if I could stand the harsh reality of my family and still receive the kind of beauty that the yard kept showing me, I would survive.

That back yard showed me how to live as it did, as a willful, driven force that carried on relentlessly with what it had to do, despite weathers or interference. Irises opened themselves up, and furry, infatuated bees rushed in. On the day after a heavy rain, a puddle appeared in a little dip in the driveway, complete with its own resident population of wriggling bugs who would vanish by afternoon when the sun extinguished the water. Once I saw a sparrow trapped in the garage, whamming itself time after time against a narrow window, even after I heaved the garage door wide open for it. That bird terrified me, for it showed me how living things will sometimes perversely refuse to choose freedom. In snow the branches of the big pine bent so low to the ground that they made a cave. When I crawled in I could see prismatic jewels that glimmered and shifted colors at the tips of the needles when I moved my head slightly.

The sparrow, the trees, the puddle, the snow crystals did not lie, and they did not expect me to lie either and agree to myself that my father would never again get drunk and hit my mother. They did not promise safety. Because I was honest like them, they told me the truth about death and ugliness and beauty, blooming and perseverance, stubbornness and letting go, all of which they lived as a matter of course. Nature, like me, absorbed it all and went on. It wasn't easy to do, but it was the secret to surviving: absorbing both the awfulness and the gorgeousness whenever and wherever they hit. My relationship with my back yard shaped my entire life. It made me a fighter always on the lookout for beauty. It insisted that, if I was brave enough to look squarely at my current reality and not only refuse to be conquered by it but to push through it to create a new reality within the prevailing and often oppressive one, then I would be gifted with wonder.

After my book about finding and making beauty in wounded places was published, people often asked me what they could do to bring on enough beauty to dispel grief. Not possible, I had to say. We must receive them both in equal measure, not sequentially but as layers that fold in and over one another: beauty and sorrow, beauty and sorrow. Beauty cannot permanently replace loss and sorrow, but it can, even when we're in the depths of grief, temporarily lift those heavy emotions just enough to get us through for a little while longer. If we are open to the possibility of receiving the simple offerings that flick and hover around our day, a feeling of astonishment will often shoot through us, like a bolt of lightning illuminating a dark sky. In that moment we are presented with a sudden, brief reveal of a world that, though it may fade quickly back to black, has imprinted on our consciousness the certainty that it did, in fact, shoot and illumine.

The challenge is to admit both grief and beauty and to recognize that we do not have to choose between them. That's not easy. The temptation may be to fall so fully under the spell of the bad stuff that there's no room for anything else, or you might turn your back on all that unpleasantness and find some way of distracting yourself from it or even disbelieving it. However, there's another temptation just as insidious: to ignore the gifts of happiness that crash through the sorrow, feeling they are somehow improper. They are not. Joy and sorrow braid together, like beauty and ugliness, like that which seduces and that which repels. To survive, to endure, to thrive is to open up to grief and beauty as fully as possible. In that way we bring more of our whole authentic human experience to life.

20. Redefine nature.

Every year conservation organizations like the Sierra Club and the Wilderness Society produce beautiful calendars with full-color photographs of nature at its most beguiling: stately pine trees reflected in clear lakes, cute baby owls in their nest, snowy mountain peaks. This nature radiates imperturbability and eternal grandeur.

But such a notion of nature is like the old matriarch of a family. She's still admired for her antique charm and elegance, but she is very much out of touch with the way the world is now. Nature at its best, according to nature calendars, is free of people. It's also immune from invasive plant and insect species. Probably it has not been scarred by fire or flood. Of course those baby owls, snowy mountains, and clear lakes are worth preserving, and the Sierra Club and Wilderness Society and many other organizations national and local do an outstanding job with that work. But real nature is not simply pristine and unpeopled wilderness, and we need to get over thinking that it is. Nature is wherever and whenever we encounter it. The outlook perpetrated by the distributors of nature calendars, that the only real nature is remote and glorious, is more common to white people who have the resources to seek out and spend time in such places, that they may garner solitude and awe. Nature is no less present and potentially awe-inspiring for people who live in the city, for those who don't have the money to get away to "pristine" nature, or even for those who don't consider themselves nature-lovers, but just can't help crunching through fallen leaves on an autumn day or sighing over a lovely sunset.

Local nature has been inspiring people for millennia, from Homer, who sang of the "rosy-fingered dawn" to Will.I.Am., who called out politicians for ignoring the danger signs of climate change in his 2007 rap song, "S.O.S. (Mother Nature)." For the Dineh people I wrote about years ago, nature (although they would never have used that isolated concept for their sacred land) was a gift from the Creator that they were entrusted to care for. "Nature" for Trayvon Martin, the African American teenager who was killed while walking home in his Florida neighborhood carrying nothing more lethal than a bag of Skittles, was his neighborhood, pointed out blogger and ecotherapist J. Phoenix Smith, where he assumed he was safe, "surrounded by familiar trees, plants."[1] "Ideas of nature never exist outside a cultural context," writes William Cronon."[2]

A goal of mine for many years was to develop some way of reuniting people with "wounded" nature, places they loved that had been damaged or destroyed by human or natural acts. I felt badly for places that people avoided or vandalized simply because they could no longer do what they used to do or look as they had previously looked. I didn't know how to go about realizing this vision, and I tried all kinds of approaches, including offering a weeklong vigil at an old-growth clear-cut forest on Vancouver Island and a day of discussion and meditation on the cloverleaf of a highway. If the offerings were free, like the ceremony I did at Ground Zero after September 11, people flocked to attend, but few, if any, signed up for the programs for which I asked a fee. Everyone understood the concept of a "wounded place." They would nostalgically recount the story of a woodland they'd played in as a child that had been bowdlerized by a golf course or a neighborhood on the Mississippi River that a petrochemical plant had gobbled up. They described their feelings of helplessness to find some way either of rescuing the place or processing their sorrow about what had happened to it. Now they just preferred to avoid those places, and they certainly didn't want to pay for the privilege of spending time with them. To me, however, it was obvious that their love for the places endured, and that the wound to the land had caused a psychic wound in them.

Psychologists remind us that we can't be whole, healthy individuals if we keep trying to cover up uncomfortable, scary feelings. Similarly, I thought, how could we foster a healthy, sustainable planet if we ignored the uncomfortable geophysical places? Honoring hurt places seemed like an important way to be in full, authentic relationship with one's territory on Earth. Finally, in 2008, I realized that many people could benefit from a practice for honoring hurt places, while helping themselves and others to do so with their financial contributions. I founded Radical Joy for Hard Times, dedicated to reuniting people with the places they have loved and lost. Since then, people around the world have been finding and making beauty in many different kinds of places that are endangered or under assault, and through that work, they are realizing that all places, like all people, have an inherent beauty and value.

When Betsy Perluss, then an associate professor of counseling at California State University, Los Angeles, received an invitation from her friend Farion Pearce to spend the morning at a contaminated metal recycling facility, she was dubious. "If I had some time off, I'd rather go hiking in a wilderness area than hang out in a dilapidated factory," she told me. But her curiosity was piqued, so on a Saturday morning in June she joined Farion and three other friends at the old Halaco plant, now an EPA Superfund site, in Oxnard. The plant had closed in 2002, and a sturdy hurricane fence barred entry to its contaminated soils, slated for EPA clean-up. They hadn't been there long when Betsy noticed that there was more to this toxic place than first met the senses. "I began to see that the factory was right next to a nesting ground for birds. All kinds of birds. It was bursting with life. I thought, *My gosh, if these birds are here, why shouldn't I be here?* I probably saw more life than I would at a wilderness place. The birds. Grass growing through the concrete. It was the surprise element that made me begin to see. If I'm hiking in the wilderness, I assume wildlife will be there. But I was surprised to see nature in a Superfund site. Then I began to fall in love with it."

Wounded, weird, or ugly nature can be fascinating as well as inspiring. My stepdaughter, Justine Gardner, told me a story about a gripping nature drama that she and her son, aged four, and a couple of other parents and children witnessed. They were in Brooklyn, New York's large and lush Prospect Park when one of the children spied a killer wasp dragging a cicada along the sidewalk. Both insects were about two inches long. The cicada was on its back, its stiff pale green legs poking into the air, one veined, diaphanous wing at its side, the other lost to the aggressions of the wasp tugging it over the rough ground. Adults and children alike stopped playing, stopped talking, and just stood and watched raptly.

When we think about redefining nature, we not only embrace the value and potential loveliness of wounded places, we also expand our very notion of nature's life. In recent years several important lawsuits have acknowledged that certain places are so valuable to their ecosystems that they have an inherent right to exist. In fact, courts in Ecuador, Bolivia, India, New Zealand, and a few U.S. states have ruled that natural features have existence, and they also have the right to persist without threat of harm. In its ruling on behalf of the Ganges and Yamuna Rivers, a court in India determined that these rivers, long sacred to humans, have "the status of a legal person, with all corresponding rights, duties and liabilities... in order to preserve and conserve them."[3] In 2019, citizens of Toledo, Ohio granted Lake Erie its own Bill of Rights and permitted any citizen to sue on behalf of the lake if they discovered actions that would pollute it. Sadly, another court invalidated the law a year later. Still, the trend toward granting rights to forces of nature evinces a growing awareness that these entities have an existence beyond any "uses" humans might want to contrive for them. Such entitlements might include the rights to flow unimpeded, to offer habitat to animal and plant species, to exist without being poisoned or blocked in its ability to be itself. The New Zealand and India laws recognize that rivers and mountains exude not only physical qualities, but spiritual ones as well. The Dineh and Hopi people I spent time with in the 1980s and early 90s would assert that it is not humans who, in some long-ago time, took it upon themselves to endow certain natural features with sanctity and animate presence, but that the canyons, springs, and mountains themselves conveyed their distinction to the people, who understood that they, in order to benefit from the blessings of these places, had a duty to take care of them. That was a requirement for being human.

For his book, *Visit Sunny Chernobyl,* Andrew Blackwell visited the most polluted places in the world, including the eponymous site in Ukraine that remains the worst nuclear disaster in history, the tarsands of Canada, and the great Pacific garbage patch. As he stares at all the wilted, snagged, washed up offerings on the Najafgarh, formerly a river, now reduced to a polluted channel draining into the sacred Yamuna River, he poses this question: "And why not? Underneath the stink and the noise, the rationale unfolded. This was a tributary of the Yamuna. Are you not to venerate it merely because it smells? Why not worship it, suspended solids and all? What could be more sacred than a river that springs from inside your neighbor's belly?"[4]

Wilderness or city park, farmland or polluted remnant of a river, bayou or small town, cicada or killer wasp—nature abides in your place: the place you're part of, the place that contains you, your landscape—wherever you are. If we think that only "pristine" nature is of value, we will overlook the nature in our midst. And if we overlook that very local, personal nature, we will fail to see and hear the many different ways that it reaches out to us, for example when a wasp drags a cicada across our path. The Sierra Club needs to rethink its lovely calendars. Each of the twelve color photographs that grace its monthly pages should include the kind of nature that surrounds us and that we are often tempted to dismiss as ordinary, or not even nature at all. A new Sierra Club calendar will feature a rose bush blooming outside a hospital, a moose strolling through a broken and abandoned building at Chernobyl, and gulls picking over their choices at a landfill. There will also be pictures of people enjoying their own local nature: small children exclaiming over a display of insect predation or a young couple lying face-up to the sun on the springtime grass of a city park. Nature has to be beautiful to us as it is today, not as it was for our grandparents or in unrealistically remote and pristine "nature" photographs. If we expect nature to meet certain lofty expectations, we might overlook a possibly more poignant nature right before our eyes.

21. Let beauty seduce you.

You know it when you see or hear or touch it, but how do you describe it? Beauty doesn't have a shape like a teapot, or a short but flashy existence like a meme. Beauty is a quality of something outside yourself that causes a reaction inside yourself. Suddenly you are magnetized to that other thing through no will of your own, but simply because of an elusive quality you know is beauty. Writing of beauty in art, Timothy Morton says "it's like finding something in me that isn't me: there is a feeling in my inner space that I didn't cook up myself, and it seems to be sent to me from this 'object' over there on the gallery wall, but when I try to find out exactly where this feeling is and what it is about the thing, or about me, that is the reason why I'm having this feelings, I can't isolate it without ruining what precisely is beautiful about it."[1] Whether the subject of your reaction is art, a human face, a horse, or an antique silk kimono, the experience you're referring to is personal to you, but at the same time it's an experience that you assume would have a similar effect on anyone else who happened to be in the presence of that face or horse or kimono.

Some artists have drawn attention to our complex relationship with beauty by choosing the ugly, the decayed, the broken, the forever-lost as the subjects of their work. A famous painting by Renaissance artist Domenico Ghirlandaio portrays a child gazing up with love at an old man who looks back at him with equal adoration. The man has a bulbous, warty nose, but that means nothing to the child, who sees only what is offered through the eyes. Love subsumes the ugly, reinvents it. As Umberto Eco has pointed out, all the millions of depictions, good and bad, trite and transcendental, of Christ on the cross are monuments to ugliness, since they call attention to suffering as a way of eliciting compassion. In the nineteenth century the Aesthetic Movement in Europe celebrated transcendental beauty in scenes of ruin, as in the German artist

Caspar David Friedrich's paintings of crumbling old churches shrouded in mist and gloom. These paintings proposed that majesty was to be found in former glory reduced to rubble. The original purpose of the buildings no longer serves, and the traces of its past, such as a shattered rose window or cracked steeple, evoke nostalgia. It doesn't matter what happened to this place. Time happened, and that's all the explanation we need. We are content with the idea of majestic decay. All things pass, we recall, as we, too, will pass, and life will go on, and beauty will not be conquered. The contemporary photographer Andrew Moore has called attention to a similar kind of mournful beauty in his shots of the abandoned, crumbling Beaux-Arts railroad station in Detroit and the relic of the once grand Ford plant—stately classical ruins, where the grandiose expectations of the builders are shown to have been betrayed by humanity's fickle passions and nature's propensity to gobble whatever it finds.

Being in the presence of beauty—*and recognizing that you are*—lifts your spirits. Beauty is medicine. Even the smallest, most ephemeral infusions of nature can sustain you at the hardest of times. Just three or four hours after my husband and I learned that bladder cancer had spread to his liver and stomach and that he had very little time left to live, I walked out of the hospital shocked, anguished, and rootless, into a hot summer afternoon. Even getting to my car seemed a monumental task. I stood there by the revolving door and whispered to something, anything. "Help. I need help." Immediately I noticed a rose bush blooming on a patch of grass between the hospital building and the sidewalk. The roses were a deep fuchsia color, and they flourished there in front of that building full of sickness and death as exuberantly if they were in a palace garden. I walked over to them, bent over one particularly resplendent flower, and inhaled deeply. The scent was cool and sweet, a precise rose emanation that would contribute its singularity into the air whether anyone noticed or not. That I had noticed and was able to receive its offering did not lessen my grief, but it did remind me of the indomitability of life. It assured me that I would survive even this devastating process and that, after Andy, and even after I too was gone, roses would survive and continue to give up their perfume to the air and to any person lucky enough to imbibe it.

Beauty is vital to sanity, because it seizes you without you having to do anything to make that body-and-mind-shaking thing happen. You are seduced, and happily, even if you're in the throes of utter misery. In *Man's Search for Meaning*, Viktor Frankl, the Austrian doctor who survived captivity in Auschwitz and the murder of his wife, mother, and brother by the Nazis, recounts a story of a man who rushed into their barracks one afternoon to urge the others to come outside quickly and see the beautiful sunset. "As the inner life of the prisoner tended to become more intense, he also experienced the beauty of art and nature as never before," Frankl wrote.[2] You can't analyze your response to beauty. You might be able to write at length about a subject of beauty, but your own reaction will remain elusive. You can't precisely locate it in your body or mind. You also can't "capture" it. Beauty is not the thing itself, it is our relationship with it.

Beauty also doesn't translate easily into a souvenir you can take back home to remind you of some real-life beauty that you experienced. The people who respond to an invitation of beauty by taking a photograph of it and then immediately walking away are making a big mistake, denying themselves a rich and textured pleasure. I've watched this folly taking place over and over at places like Strasbourg Cathedral in France, the Monet waterlilies at the Museum of Modern Art in New York, and the statue of the golden Buddha in Bangkok. People walk up to a thing, recognize it as wondrous, take a picture, and move on. They are noting beauty, acknowledging it for what is, and then refusing to be seduced by it. Only by standing still for beauty can you be properly and thoroughly seduced. Those who bypass the physical response to beauty and simply take a picture are assuming that a photograph, which they may or may not even look at later on, is as poignant and authentic as the real thing. It's not. It's a copy, a thread from the tapestry, the plastic bride and groom from the top of the wedding cake. It's like reading the words "statue of Buddha" and believing you're standing before a gently smiling thirty-foot-long reclining figure of pure gold. Actually, the real bloom on your Christmas cactus is more beautiful than a photograph of the golden Buddha, because it entices you with an immediate, bodily experience.

You can't make beauty appear to you, but you can be open to it, so you don't miss it when it happens to shoot its Eros-arrow your way. We have to track beauty and grab it when it winks at us! Grabbing the beauty that shoots through brokenness and taking the risk to pass it on might just save the Earth—or at least our life on Earth.

22. Transcend downward.

Who doesn't want to get beyond the sorrows and indignities that weigh us down every day? Who among us hasn't thought that, If only this one thing were different, then my whole life would be different and I would be able, finally, to live as I was meant to. It doesn't matter if you believe in God or not, reincarnation or not, heaven or not, where you are here on the Earth is sometimes a very weighty and difficult place to be stuck in. You long for something different. You want to be something different. The scholar of myth and religion, Mircea Eliade, wrote, "The desire to free himself from his limitations, which he feels to be a kind of degradation, and to regain spontaneity and freedom... must be ranked among the specific marks of man."[1] We long to transcend, Eliade wrote, and by "transcend" he means to be wrenched free of our earthly concerns and become other than a mere body, not because we can think or even act our way out of that physical state, but because we have somehow surpassed it. It just no longer matters quite so much.

When we think of "transcending," we usually think of being lifted to some higher realm. Yet expecting that kind of transcendence is like hoping that someone else will come along and fix something we can't. It's waiting for God, the right medicine that will cure us, or the right romantic partner to materialize and elope with us out of the here and now into a happier there and then. A more reliable way of transcending is to transcend downward. I mean, to lose ourselves and temporarily divert our immediate woes by letting the world itself, not God, seize, stun, and enlighten us.

During a Zoom meeting in the first month of the coronavirus pandemic, a colleague in New York City gasped in the middle of a conversation. He had been arguing for a certain approach to fundraising, but suddenly he said, "Oh, wow, wait a second." We all waited, wondering a bit nervously after he stood up from his desk and disappeared from view. Soon he was back. "Oh, my god, I can't believe what just happened. A flock of seagulls flew right down the middle of West 49th Street! And then, at the corner, they all turned right and headed down Eighth Avenue. The firefighters came out from their station to watch!"

The anthropologist and essayist Loren Eiseley once mused that the most beautiful sight in the world might be "birds taking over New York as the last man has run away to the hills."[2] Humans were not running to the hills on that day in April 2020, but they had vacated the streets to such an extent that the birds did seem to be taking over spaces formerly occupied by honking taxis, the crosstown bus, and a steady stream of pedestrians in a hurry. My colleague and the firefighters were allured out of the ordinary into something strange and beguiling, much like the woodcutter in the Swedish fable who is chopping wood in a cold and lonely forest when a magical woman, Hulda, appears and smiles at him. Immediately he is compelled to drop his ax and follow her, though she may never again turn to face him. The message is clear: what matters is accepting the invitation to transcend when it presents itself, not wasting time by pondering where the invitation might lead. When my colleague and those firefighters were transported by the sight of seagulls reclaiming the streets of New York, they allowed themselves to grab the light in the dark. They could have stifled their response of delight. My colleague might have kept expounding on his convictions about fundraising, and the firefighters might simply have glanced out and glanced back to whatever quiet activity they were engaged in on a morning when no emergency demanded their intervention. Instead, they all succumbed to wonder. They let the Earth grab them. They transcended downward.

It might be a dose of beauty that invites you to transcend, or it might be something else, something you overhear, something odd you have to stop and look at, or some collision of your own thought of the moment and an event nearby that seems to have been preordained to come together just for your enlightenment. The journey of transcending downward begins with the thing that calls, but it is your own willingness to be swept away that gives it momentum. You don't need drugs or alcohol to transcend downward. In fact, external mood-changers only render you more reliant on props to sweep you away, so you miss those invitations that beckon you in your perfectly ordinary moments. The person who takes a photograph of the Golden Buddha and then walks away without stopping to be drawn in by it is bypassing beauty—and also shunning the opportunity to transcend.

The purpose of transcending downward is not to attain enlightenment or understand at last the true nature of God. It's to become part of something larger than yourself, something that, once you find yourself there, turns out to have been saving a place for exactly your kind of circumstances, your kind of sensibility. Momentarily you give up the struggle. You surrender to the mystery of the wondrous. You are washed through with a sense of the rightness of all things, including your own unhappiness, your desperation, your frustration, your impatience. You are able to say to yourself, *Yes, it belongs. It all belongs, And I, too, I belong.* Unless you are a religious mystic, your moments of transcendence will be brief. They will nevertheless be profound.

Often, when those moments of uplift occur, our inclination is not to greet them, but rather to shove them away. We dismiss them as inappropriate, as though grief and anxiety alone have the right to claim this stage in our life right now and must be allowed their full, uninterrupted soliloquy. Maybe we fear that by permitting ourselves that drop into amazement, we will be disloyal to other suffering people. Or we worry that by tumbling, even for a moment, into the arms of happiness, we'll lose our credibility as a suffering person, along with the expressions of sympathy that accompany it.

But those instants of capture by rapture aren't wrong or rude or selfish, they're medicine from the great mystery of life and that part of the human spirit that refuses to die. They are outrageous gifts of grace in hard times, and we are fools not to grasp hold of them with all our might. They can't change circumstances, but they can utterly change our relationship with those circumstances. They remind us that our human sensibility is quirky and complex, and they tug us to participate more fully and playfully in that quirkiness, that complexity. Moments of uplift jog our consciousness into that old truth we knew as children without ever having to think about it—that we are, each of us, endowed with a mysterious, easily accessible, and intimate connection with this world, and that magic can pop up and amaze us at any time.

Widening our spiritual aperture to receive the light in the dark also means deliberately conjuring gratitude during hard times. Gratitude brings balance to a situation, and it's the small things we take for granted that are the most accessible items for a list of simple bounties: *It felt good to walk into the warmth of this shelter on a cold day, even if it is only temporary and I have no idea where I will live next. My child came safely home from school this afternoon with a painting she made. I just discovered a Valentine my husband had been making for me and never completed, and it is like a love note after his death. In this burned forest, green shoots of growth are already pushing through the char.* Viktor Frankl relates the little spurt of happiness that the Jewish concentration camp prisoners would occasionally receive at mealtime. The soup they were served was tasteless and watery, yet anyone who happened to get one of the last servings, scraped from the bottom of the pot, might find, like a special gift, a whole pea or two in the bottom of their bowl. Gratitude, ferreted out and named, can pierce the darkness, becoming itself like a moment of beauty. Sometimes allowing ourselves to be seized by astonishment is the most appropriate response to the moment.

My friend Rachel told me of a weekend trip to Vermont that she took with her sister in the fall of 2019, days after four people had been stabbed in Paris, North Korea had launched a ballistic missile, protestors were continuing to gather in Hong Kong, and concerns were building after a whistleblower who worked in the White House revealed that Donald Trump had tried to coerce Ukrainian president Zelensky to investigate Joe Biden's son. The two women stopped at a maple syrup farm and had a chat with the owners about what weather patterns are best for tapping the sugar maples and how the syrup changes flavor and richness the more it's cooked. Rachel bought bottles of syrup and maple candies. She felt happy to have met interesting people and learned more about the process that begins with trees in late winter and results in sweetness for the human body. But when they got back into the car, her sister complained, "How can you enjoy talking about maple syrup when the whole world is in such a mess?"

Actually, this is exactly the right time to talk about maple syrup, just as it was exactly the time for my colleague to absent himself momentarily from our Zoom meeting to watch an avian takeover of West 49th Street. Seagulls and maple syrup cannot immunize a person against the coronavirus, cure disease, run a bad leader out of office, or reverse climate change. But they are gifts of grace that we receive without having to do anything to "earn" them. They arrive and greet us and then, typically, they dissipate. They remind us that there is stubborn resilience in the world, even when we, mere mortal human beings, feel weak, powerless, and despondent. They bestow on us a moment of wonder when we least expect it. They transform the ordinary into something magical and extraordinary.

As we learn to co-exist in the age of climate change and pandemic, we realize that we cannot be truly generous and brave until we honestly face all aspects of our human sensibility and the body of the Earth, ask what they have to teach us, and welcome the ones that engender awe, inspiration, resilience, and a sense of oneness with the greater whole of life. In order to fully live in this challenging world, where so much of the beauty and diversity, the routine and regularity we once took for granted is being snatched away from us, it is essential to risk being swept up by the fleet, the mysterious, the illogical, and the purely magical. Author Neil Evernden told an interviewer that, after writing two books on the human relationship with nature, what he really began to care about was the "shock of the other.... the shock of encountering a frog or a cat or just listening at a frog pond.... I view it not as an expansion of self but a loss of self."[3] The ability to be staggered by the world's minutiae is a gift at any time. It can feel like a life-saver in hard times. The "loss of self" Evernden advocates is not frightening and limiting, but rather freeing. To deny ourselves the fullness of rapture for fear that the thing that transports us will compromise our rational minds is to deny ourselves life. It is to close off all kinds of byways in the human psyche and block off mysterious experiences that could just possibly motivate us to care, to protect, to act, to create.

The words *catastrophe* and *cataclysm* root in the Greek *kata*, meaning "down." Catastrophe means a "turn downward" and cataclysm, which originally referred to flooding, was a "washing down." We need a new word, something like "catalume," that would irradiate that downward motion with the addition of the Latin word *luminosis*, meaning "shining, full of light." It is possible to gain light in the darkness, and to be uplifted—or rather "downdrawn"—if we succumb to the magic that wants to enchant us.

The poet, essayist, and farmer Wendell Berry writes:

> "Your hope of Heaven, let it rest
> on the ground underfoot."[4]

Let there be catalume!

23. Open up to the marvel of others.

The practice of thriving through hard times mandates that, even as I recognize the sorrows of other people and exercise compassion, I must also be on the lookout for what is intriguing, brave, and adorable about them. Opening up to the marvel of others makes the world a lot more interesting. It connects you with people, encourages others to show you their better selves, and brings you out of your own doldrums.

It's easy to regard a person's outer appearance as infallible evidence of their whole, authentic self. I might even assume that someone whose political, religious, racial, or economic composition differs from mine must be wholly opposite from me in every respect. In that case, I might be tempted to avoid those people. But humans are variegated and complex, with all kinds of possible points of intersection. Sometimes they're obvious, often they're not. A woman who lived down the road from me lost her husband just few weeks after Andy died. Previously our interactions had been limited to waves and greetings when I passed by their house on one of my walks, and she and her husband were sitting on their porch. I had always admired the garden she'd made in the tiny patch of their front lawn, profuse with delphiniums, roses, beebalm, and sunflowers, but we'd never had a real conversation. Perhaps we supposed we had little in common, for every four years the signs staked in their front lawn touted one presidential candidate, while the ones in ours championed his opponent.

But after we became widows, political differences collapsed into the shared reality of grief. Suddenly we knew things about each other that we had never shared. Standing in front of the post office in our masks or talking across her garden, we skipped surface pleasantries and spoke about the heartbreaking business of caring for the one you love when he is suffering, about the anguish of entering your home for the first time after he has died, about being thrust into a caste of loneliness for which no amount of projection or spiritual faith has prepared you. "No one else can understand what it is to go through this," she said to me on an icy gray afternoon as she twined Christmas lights around the railing of her porch. By then, we weren't ignoring each other's political preferences; they just didn't matter. We were two women cohering over the death of the person we had loved most in the world. Sunk in loneliness and grief, we touched one other person treading those same waters. I would say we felt, during those conversations, if not love for each other, then profound empathy as we reached out to grab the hand of another survivor floating on the jetsam after a big storm. We knew so little about our individual lives, yet we understood each other utterly.

It's not necessary to dig determinedly around in somebody's psyche in order to find those places of intersection. This is not an exercise in developing sleuthing skills. Unlike learning from an unexpected teacher, such as the young woman I saw tenderly ministering to an old, sick man in a subway station, this practice isn't ingesting some useful tip that you can adapt in your own life. It's about connecting with another human being long enough to recognize something interesting or admirable about them. A question I like to ask people is what they love about something they do, whether it's knitting or chopping wood or doing laser surgery on people's eyes. So often, upon first meeting someone, we ask, "What do you do?" Then maybe you mutter a little lilting "Oh" in response, as if to communicate that that's very interesting, thank you very much. After that the conversation often stalls. Finding out why they do what they do, whether it's a profession or a hobby, brings the energy out of people. They reveal who they really are by talking about what they really love to somebody who's apparently interested.

The French surrealist André Breton had a different all-revealing question in mind to ask a stranger. In his novel, *Nadja*, about the woman he encountered at a Paris bookstall who enthralled him and became his lover, he describes this "one question which sums up all the rest, a question which only I would ever ask, probably, but which has at least once found a reply worthy of it: 'Who are you?' And she, without a moment's hesitation: 'I am the soul in limbo.'"[1] For Breton, Paul Eluard, Marcel Duchamps and the other French surrealists of the early twentieth century, any encounter had the potential to be marvelous. And so many of them were.

The French-Lithuanian philosopher Emmanuel Levinas was preoccupied with the primary experience of co-existence and how to meet it "face-to-face." For Levinas, the seed of compassion becomes embedded in us when we truly see the face of the other. In every face, he says, there is a plea: "Do not hurt me!" It's easy to overlook that cry—for understanding, for sympathy, for appreciation—especially when I encounter someone whose inner universe I have presumed to comprehend based on a quick assessment of their outer appearance or circumstances. When I watch a movie star on TV as she glides along the red carpet into the Academy Awards ceremony, or when I pass a man in ragged clothes sitting on a city sidewalk with a cardboard sign professing his homelessness, I tend to assemble a quick inner portrait of who they are. The actress thinks she's someone special; she disdains ordinary people like me; she has everything. The homeless man possibly did something wrong that led to his predicament; he is dirty; he might try to steal from me. Levinas, like filmmaker Andi Olsen, invites me to recognize that each has a face, and each face has a need. Olsen's film shows you where the smiling fades down. The smiling fades up when people talk about what they love.

24. Play.

Once I saw a photograph of Palestinian children playing in the wreckage of a building in the Gaza Strip that had been demolished by an Israeli missile. The building was so damaged that you could not have identified what its former purpose might have been. It was just big chunks of white stone toppled over one another to create a hodgepodge of angles and gaps. Behind it another building remained upright, though one wall had blown off, leaving a jagged hole. The children were exploring the possibilities of this field of novelty, this familiar world rearranged. They climbed the stones, slid down on their backsides, crawled in and out of the gaping spaces.

Do you remember what it was like to be a child encountering a world rearranged? A large, empty cardboard box from a new refrigerator, a tree uprooted by storm, snow metamorphosing your neighborhood—when we saw those transformed landscapes, we felt a sizzle of excitement: *What possibilities are here in this new world? How might I enter in and make this gift into something all my own?* The psychologist D.W. Winnicott was fascinated with play—what motivates it, how it unfolds, how children pick up objects and begin to imagine them anew. Play allows us to feel kinship with the other as we discover a new creation of the self, Winnicott wrote. The things we play with, from dolls to toy guns to playing "house," enable us to move about, inventing all the way, in both the real world and a made-up world at the same time. Out of the unfamiliar we create the familiar. Out of the familiar we create the unfamiliar. We discover new aspects of our selves. We make priorities. "Play is children's language," writes Kate Cray in *The Atlantic*. "They act out pretend scenarios as a way to express concerns, ask questions, and, crucially, reshape a narrative. In a pretend scenario, children are driving the plot and can change the outcome of a scary situation or try out different solutions to a problem."[1] She cites the example of a group of children who incorporated and challenged the restrictions of COVID-19 by inventing a safely distanced game of tag in which they would tag someone by stepping on their shadow.

It's not always easy for adults to re-enter the magical world of play, despite their good intentions. Sometimes the people who came to the rites of passage programs I led would declare firmly that they were going to devote part of their solo time in the wilderness to "playing," because they felt they had become too serious, and they wanted to recapture some of the spontaneity and creativity of their childhood. But when they were alone and set about to perform this task they'd assigned themselves, they found it was just that—a task—and they were flummoxed. They didn't know how to proceed. Should they set up some "toys" made of pinecones and sticks and then move them around? Recreate a game they dimly remembered from their childhood? They felt embarrassed about their awkwardness and confirmed in their belief that they had lost the knack of play.

It is especially difficult for adults to engage in creative play if they have been traumatized. In that case, says psychologist Robert Landry, they can begin to rediscover play by "sparring with language, telling stories, playing out alternative scenarios in thought, even meditating."[2] When they're comfortable with these mental and verbal excursions into the imagination, they may be able to play roles, build things, and in this way "experience a sense of control and balance."

Actually, it's possible to play with any thing at any time, as the Palestinian children re-inventing their upturned world demonstrate so clearly. In the 1990s, when I was writing about the Dineh (Navajo) and Hopi people, I went to a coffee shop in Window Rock, on Dineh land, with two elderly sisters and the little granddaughter, about four years old, of one of them. While we adults talked, the child was completely immersed in enacting a quiet drama on the table with a stub of pencil and a spoon. For an adult, too, anything can serve as a prop or a prompt for play. You can play at washing the dishes, starting, say, with the smallest dirty object you can find and scrubbing your way up to the largest. You can play when you shovel snow, digging your way through the drifts in spirals or mazes instead of just trudging down a straight line. When you go to the supermarket, you can give your cart a little extra push and hitch a ride on it as you make your way down an empty aisle. If you're a reader, you can go to your bookcase, close your eyes, pick a book at random and open it up, then read a paragraph or two and pierce your routine with some plot or piece of information you had had no plan to explore that day.

Radical Joy for Hard Times events always conclude with the participants making a gift for their wounded place out of materials the place itself offers. This is important. It reminds everyone that we have at hand whatever we need to make beauty, even at the site of an underground coal fire or a vacant, littered lot or any other place that has undergone human or natural calamity. We also urge each person to join in the making of this gift. Some people demure: "I'm not creative, I'm not an artist." But then they pick up a stick, a stone, a bright scarlet leaf, and they add it to the co-created offering. It seems a small action, but it engages the entire group, whether two people or fifty, in the act of making something new and meaningful out of a ground where nothing but destruction was before. The overall condition of the place remains unchanged, but the relationship that the people have with it has undergone a transformation—and each person present has had a hand in making that happen.

At one of our annual Global Earth Exchanges, Lucy Hinton and her friends met in London's Clissold Park with the intention of bringing a little wildness into the stuffiness of urban life. "England is being increasingly strangled by a culture of restriction, red tape & paranoid regulation," Lucy had written us. "A generation of children are growing up metaphorically wrapped in suffocating cotton wool, distanced from the opportunity to develop their own survival instincts & their own genuine creative strengths." The playful mission got off to a good start when one of the young men arrived for the event attired in a formal business jacket, while his face was painted in Earth-invoking colors of green and blue. While a ladybird sang nearby, the group sat in a circle on the grass and shared stories of the wildness they remembered and their sadness at how much of it was disappearing. Then everyone went off to explore and find beauty. Lucy and another friend were inspired to climb the fences that had been installed to keep people away from the lakes and to pick up the litter there. After doing their good deed—and being noticed then left quite alone by a passing policeman—she snatched some actual red tape from around the fence, and everyone used it to make our symbol, the RadJoy Bird.

When we allow ourselves to be immersed in the world before us purely for the sake of immersion, without having to learn, clean, repair, or improve, a sense of intimacy with our surroundings springs up. Forms that seemed, just moments ago, purely functional or simply part of the background begin to metamorphose and show themselves as quirky beings that want to cajole us to get more deeply involved with them. Immersion in the duologue reminds us how possible it is to dissolve boundaries between me and not-me. Play opens us up to interacting with this delightful other in a way that is impractical, temporary, and even fun.

25. Inquire into the mystery of objects coming alive.

When he was a little boy, Shaka Fumu Kabaka witnessed the atrocities that shook his home town of Kisangani, Democratic Republic of Congo during the six-day war between Rwanda and Uganda in 2000. Although his own country was not directly involved, more than a thousand people were killed there, and the memory of seeing the blood and the bodies of so many people during those days stayed with Kabaka as he grew up. Now he has become part of Ndaku Ya La Vie Est Belle, a collective of artists in the capital city of Kinshasa, who are pointing up social and ecological troubles through wearable art they make from ordinary objects. Attired in costumes they've conjured from rubbish and walking through the city streets, they shock, disturb, inform, and engage people wherever they go.

As they educate others about pressing issues, these artists are also coming to come to terms with their own grief. Kabaka's costume is called Matshozi 6 Jours (Six Days of Tears). He made it out of broken dolls that he scavenged over a period of more than a year from household rubbish. "The first time I wore the costume, it was a heavy burden," he told a reporter. "Not because of the weight, but because of the number of casualties it represents." Street performer Falonne Mambu designed Femme Électrique (Electric Woman) out of electric wire. "In the dark, the residents dare not come out of their houses," she said. "If there were light, social control would be greater, more people would be on the street. What I experienced on the streets of Kinshasa as a homeless young woman and what many girls still experience today I address through my paintings and performances. I can talk about sexual violence through my work." [1] Another found-object apparition that has wandered the city is Kalenga Kabangu Jared's cloak of broken radio parts, which he created to call attention to the cacophony of fake news.

The objects these artists have scavenged and repurposed are still what they were originally, but now they have become something else in addition. They have become art, they have become costume, they have become reminders of violence and its effect on the psyche. A rubber baby doll head smeared with red paint and dangling from a long cloak retains little of the innocence it had when it was attached to a rubber body and was loved by a child. Now it has gained complexity and a troubling history. Objects like these, which lose simple definitions the more you study them, are the subject of an odd branch of philosophy called Object Oriented Ontology (OOO), which views objects as individual entities with complicated, individual existences in the world. Both the living and the nonliving are of interest to OOO thinkers, because to them every single thing has a being that is tangled and far-flung, beyond complete understanding. One of the founders of this perspective, Graham Harman, writes that OOO philosophers share "enjoyment at the thought that electrical and geological facts are permeated by deeper metaphysical vibrations. Some have also noticed a similar upbeat irreverence in our writings." He describes this worldview as an "uncompromising realism. The world is not the world as manifest to humans; to think a reality beyond our thinking is not nonsense, but obligatory."[2]

It's easy to make fun of OOO: Is the cheese on your grilled cheese sandwich a discrete object, or is it entangled in the greater object of the sandwich itself? Nevertheless, this perspective invites us to think about the aliveness and intricacy of the world in new ways. Just as the artists of Ndaku Ya La Vie Est Belle see dolls and circuit boards as the raw materials for a socially-conscious garment, when we consider the life of things and their connections and all we do not know about them, and when we speculate about the past and future of those objects, the world bursts open in new ways. After all, we really do have a relationship with the objects in our midst, and we are implicated in their secret lives. Have you ever lost your glasses or a favorite piece of jewelry and been filled with dread and sadness, almost as if the thing had been kidnapped and was possibly being mistreated somewhere beyond your care? When I lose something, I often have the sense that it was not my own carelessness that resulted in the disappearance of my now increasingly valued thing, but some perverse willfulness on the part of the object itself, which has simply gotten up from the desk or counter where I left it and struck out on its own. And then, when you have suddenly found that object, did you not feel a rush of relief? Did you not pick it up with a sense of welcoming love, because the object has made its way back home to you? Even when these objects are not on your body or in your immediate thoughts—when they are calmly lying in their place, awaiting your return—they are having their own existence. They are gathering dust, being knocked over by a cat, getting tangled with other pieces of jewelry in your drawer. They are not constantly in your control.

The whole world waits to be discovered and acknowledged. It waits to be listened to. Rivers speak. Flocks of birds tell one another, and those who know how to translate their language, whether a hawk is enroute into the sky overhead or a cat is on the prowl, whether there is a source of food in some human's yard or whether one's mate is in a nearby tree. The grass and the leaves speak when the wind blows and the rain falls. Even rock speaks to and quivers with its environment. In 2018 scientists attached seismic recording equipment to Castleton Tower, a stately formation of redrock presiding over the Utah desert. The rock, they discovered, hums in a low and varying tone that sounds like a cross between a whale's song and the drone of a jetliner. Every now and then the tone skips or wavers, as if something has happened to it. And, yes, something has happened. Castleton Tower, which vibrates at about the same frequency as a human heartbeat, is responding to wind, distant tremors in the earth, heat and cold, and even passing cars. "We like to think of it as a voice," said Dr. Jeff Moore, one of the geologists who is monitoring that and other rock formations. "It's sort of alive with this vibrational energy."[3]

Making friends with objects is very relevant to how we might live with climate change as once familiar things like springtime, the Alps, and lakes radically shift out of the previous forms we have casually associated with them. I myself learned a lot about getting to know the unseen beneath the familiar when I started taking walks in a former coal mining area in northeastern Pennsylvania, about twenty-five miles south of my home. The town of Olyphant had been at the uppermost tip of the state's anthracite coal fields, a swath comprising the largest deposits of this hard, pure, high-heat coal in all the Americas. Although the industry had ended six decades earlier, the life of the coal was everywhere, sometimes in grotesquely visible form, sometimes completely hidden. It appeared before me as a big pile of coal debris, called a culm, just off the road, a black hill glittering like obsidian in the late afternoon sun. As I walked past it up a dirt track, I noted the sudden presence of coal when the soil under my boots changed from a powdery dough color to gritty black. This shift was an infallible sign that under my feet stretched the remnants of a seam of coal. Still deeper down were the labyrinthine underground passageways constructed in a pattern called "room-and-pillar." The "rooms" were spaces cut into the rock, while the "pillars" were those parts of the substratum left untouched, so as to keep the whole architecture from collapsing. The miners worked these tunnels ten hours a day six days a week. When a man died in the mine, his body would be dumped in front of the small house he rented from the coal company. Everyone in the family knew that if they didn't find a replacement for him within a few days, they'd be kicked out of their home. Little boys as young as seven worked as "breakers" for pennies a week, bent over piles of black rock that mounted before them as they sorted the lumps into different sizes and picked out the waste. Up a steep, stony, rutted former road, a hurricane fence blocked off an area where an underground coal fire had been burning for sixteen years. When I hovered my hand over the gap between two rocks, I could feel the heat emanating from the mines.

So here at this place, lovely and inviting on a fall afternoon, with dragonflies swooping over a black lacquer pond, ash and beech trees turning gold and scarlet, and ravens playing in the blue sky, here the ground harbored a secret underground life. The tunnels themselves, now empty and damp, held within their architecture hard times, loss, poverty, anxiety, lasting friendships, and loyalty. My curiosity about the place expanded the more I spent time there. I noticed how certain areas had turned into dumps for trash. Some people had gone out of their way to take their empty paint cans, old tires, a child's plastic pedal car, and clots of fused stuff up to this waste place and leave it there, for, it seems, that which is considered waste calls to itself yet more waste. I noticed bear scat and the bizarre loveliness of stunted poplar trees with their sun-colored leaves shoving out of the bright black coal Earth. Each time I was there I left a gift for the place, weaving dried flowers and leaves into the hurricane fence or making a bird on the road out of chunks of coal.

Joanna Macy teaches that paying attention to the life of objects is, in some cases, not just an interesting philosophical play activity but a matter of survival. She has proposed a long-term, community-wide vigil, the Nuclear Guardianship Project, to be undertaken by people who live near nuclear power plants or waste storage facilities. These projects would begin in the present day and extend thousands of generations into the future, as people take it upon themselves to monitor undead plutonium while its lethality slowly fades in a half-life of twenty thousand years. The work of the nuclear guardians would be social, cultural, and spiritual. People would monitor the facilities to assure that they meet health and safety standards, and they would make sure that the stories of nuclear waste and its threat to life are passed down, so that no one forgets the danger of the substance to which they are bearing witness. They would also bring spiritual mindfulness to the work by holding vigils at the facility, offering songs and prayers, and dancing the story of a natural element of the Earth made deadly.

Climate change will force us to rethink the way we relate to many objects. Lakes will dry up, and then how long will we continue to call them "lakes"? The manually operated can opener that seems laughably old-fashioned to us now might be a life-saver when fire or flood has extinguished the electrical grids. The song, "White Christmas," which already sounds nostalgic, will be as mythic a concept as the rows of stately elm trees we hear once lined the streets of American towns. What we think we know will be unreliable, while the strange and familiar becomes helpful in bizarre ways. In the movie *Wall-E*, after all, it's a couple of robots who save the world.

26. Bear witness.

When I think about "receiving," I tend to imagine being the recipient of something welcome and friendly, such as a gift or a compliment or a refund. But if I am to survive and even prevail in difficult times, I must be willing to accept a heavier kind of bestowal as well. I must bear witness. In other words, I must open up to receiving some of the suffering of others. That doesn't mean that I immerse myself so completely in another's state of unhappy affairs that I become incapacitated. It means, rather, that I take in the truth of someone's hard situation, hang out with it, soak it in as the soil receives the rain, rather than just giving it a quick nod before I move along to something more pleasurable. This matter of being present for the reality of another is different from refusing to disbelieve, the first suggestion in this book. Refusing to disbelieve means accepting a difficult reality. Bearing witness means keeping a steady eye on that reality as it affects others besides myself. It means taking in that reality and responding appropriately. Bearing witness is made both harder and easier by the fact that I am not necessarily under any obligation to change the situation before me. It's easier because I can simply absorb; I do not have to distract myself from the experience by contemplating what my reactions might or ought to be. It's harder, however, because I must allow my consciousness to do just that, to *simply absorb*, without hastening to contrive solutions that will fix the wrong for the injured party and assuage feelings of powerlessness and discomfort in myself.

The definition of "to bear witness" is to indicate awareness that something has happened. My friend and colleague Harriet Sams, an archeopsychologist, who studies the way landscapes have affected cultures, says that bearing witness makes her a part of something, and when she is part, she cannot help feeling an emotional attachment to that place, person, or event. If you acknowledge yourself as a witness, you take on a bit of what has occurred in your presence. You incorporate it into your experience. Witnessing a serious car accident on the road you're driving is a lot different from merely watching a car crash in a film. Witnessing has put the event in your blood like a mineral your system isn't familiar with. What you do with that event, that strange mineral is another question.

Sometimes bearing witness means going public with what you've observed. Court trials depend on witnesses to offer up testimony of what they have personally seen or heard at the time a crime was committed, and what they reveal can dramatically affect the outcome of a trial. For the poet Wislawa Szymborska, writing of the atrocious conditions at a Nazi prisoner of war camp in Jaslo, in her native Poland, witnessing was the only way to honor the lives of those who had suffered. She exhorts herself to see, remember, and to find a way to air it all:

> Write it. Write. In ordinary ink
> on ordinary paper: they were given no food,
> they all died of hunger. "All. How many?
> It's a big meadow. How much grass
> for each one?" Write I don't know.
> History counts its skeletons in round numbers.[1]

That "ordinary ink" is the expression of a truth. The poet vows to root herself in what happened and not turn away toward the comforting abstractions of historical records or find a euphemism for the place behind the barricades where the Polish prisoners were crowded and where, in desperation, they resorted to eating grass and dirt. She cannot know all the individual lives of those who took their last breaths there, but she refuses to mass all those lives into a convenient statistic. Susan Sontag wrote, "The gruesome invites us to be either spectators or cowards, unable to look."[2] To witness is not just to look but to take in. A witness is more than a spectator; a witness shares the burden.

Witnessing can be serious business. A witness to the signing of a document attests to its binding nature. In legal descriptions of places, corners are sometimes identified by a specific landmark called a "witness monument," such as a tree, boulder, or bridge. "Here there is the sense of the permanence, of the eternal and unwavering truth of the witnessing as a legal and moral fact," wrote lawyer Thomas A. Dooling in an essay for *Parabola* Magazine. In old England a "witness tree" could not be cut down.[3] Bearing witness can also be dangerous. It can make you unpopular and, in extreme cases, even put your life at risk. Whistleblowers who dare to witness and report on unethical activities in their workplace are condemned by employers and praised by the public. Most of them have wrestled with their conscience for months or years before making their report, and they know that the consequences of doing so will be dramatic and possibly harmful. The United States Witness Protection Program recognizes the gravity of agreeing to testify to the details of a crime and provides some witnesses with new identities and homes in distant cities, that they might escape the revenge of those whose misdeeds they have dared to name.

Witnessing can also lead to despair. In 1993, the front page of the *New York Times* featured a photograph by Kevin Carter of a tiny, emaciated Sudanese child crouched on parched ground, her legs too spindly to lift her body, her head sunk down on the dirt. Just a few feet behind the child, a plump vulture stands in wait. Although Carter won a Pulitzer Prize for the photograph, he took his own life three months later, leaving behind a note in which he named debt, depression, and memories of starving children as reasons for his desperate state of mind. After this photograph had been published and republished around the world, Carter had been widely criticized for documenting the moment instead of helping the child. He had admitted that he'd even waited there on the scene in hopes that the vulture would open its wings, making it look even more predatory for the camera. Yet the photograph itself bore stunning witness to the plight, not just of that one child, but to the twenty thousand other people who died during the famine.

Not all testimony we receive is meant to be shared. Sometimes, in fact, just the opposite is the right response. After Hurricane Katrina tore through New Orleans, Abraham Verghese, a physician from San Antonio, went to the city to volunteer his medical services. In the beginning, in an effort to be polite and show concern, he had asked his patients how they had spent their days since the levees flooded the town. "But as the night wore on," he wrote, "I understood that they *needed* me to ask; to not ask was to not honor their ordeal. Hard men wiped at their eyes and became animated in the telling. The first woman, the one who seemed mute from stress, began a recitation in a courtroom voice, as if preparing for future testimony." Hearing these sometimes desperate stories made Verghese rethink his purpose for being there in New Orleans:

> It reminded me of my previous work in field clinics in India and Ethiopia, where, with so few medical resources at hand, the careful listening, the thorough exam, the laying of hands was the therapy. And I felt the same helplessness, knowing that the illness here was inextricably linked to the bigger problem of homelessness, disenfranchisement and despair. Driving home I remembered my own metaphor of strapping on armor for the night shift. The years have shown that there is no armor. There never was. The willingness to be wounded may be all we have to offer.[4]

In this case, the definition of bearing witness, "to show signs of what happened," is simply to listen fully, patiently, openly, without making judgment or offering advice.

"The willingness to be wounded may be all we have to offer," Verghese wrote. Why would we deliberately offer ourselves up to being wounded? Because doing so might soothe the pain of someone who is more critically wounded. After Andy died, I told the story of his last days over and over again to my friends. Relating the narrative accomplished several things that I could in no way have enumerated at the time. It made the finality of my beloved's death

127

real. It etched into my memory an experience of the sacred passageway from life into no-life, a profound teaching about all of existence. It reminded me that I had many friends who loved me and were willing to share my experience, even though the restrictions of the pandemic kept us physically apart. And, what I didn't realize for several months, was that it also told me that I could not only endure but mindfully navigate the worst scenario I could have imagined, and that made me believe I could move forward into a life without Andy.

It's hard to bear witness. Some people just can't take it, Sontag noted, because the suffering of another makes them, the witness, suffer too. Every participant in a program I led for people with life-altering illnesses said that one of the hardest parts of being sick was that some of their friends simply abandoned them. "They couldn't take it," said one woman, who had a rare bone disease. The philosopher Simone Weil believed that the yearning to avoid the extreme suffering of others is due to our awareness that calamity could happen to us ourselves at any time. To witness suffering is to get too close to something that could be horribly contagious. "To acknowledge the reality of affliction," Weil wrote, "means saying to oneself: 'I may lose at any moment, through the play of circumstances over which I have no control, anything whatsoever that I possess, including those things which are so intimately mine that I consider them as being myself. There is nothing that I might not lose. It could happen at any moment that what I am might be abolished and replaced by anything whatsoever of the filthiest and most contemptible sort."[5] When suffering people see others turn away from them, they can't help but wonder if they themselves have become, through their misfortune, filthy and contemptible.

But bearing witness is especially important in times of crisis. One of the hallmarks of Black Lives Matter has been the insistence that white people stop talking and presuming and deciding so much and simply listen. It is time for African Americans to tell their stories and voice their opinions without interruption, defensiveness, or dismissal, expressions of free speech that they have been denied, directly or indirectly, for four hundred years in the United States. Climate change will also invite opportunities to bear witness in the way Abraham Verghese described. As solastalgia, or homesickness for the home they've lost to wildfire, hurricanes, mudslides, or tornados, radically shifts how we live, we and our neighbors and the strangers we'll encounter will all need to come to grips with our experience in some way that will enable us to carry on. Having someone to tell our story to will be essential. Listening with patience and compassion will be essential. And in hard times our stories need to be told more than once, for every telling strips off another layer of isolation. A woman who lost her home in one of California's devastating wildfires told me that she got into the habit of riding her bike through the cindered, unrecognizable streets of her former neighborhood. Whenever she met another person, she would stop, and they would exchange stories. Those visits and conversations became a spiritual practice for her.

We can bear witness not only to hurt people but to hurt places as well, for they, too, tell their stories. At the National Memorial for Peace and Justice that opened in Birmingham, Alabama in 2018, hundreds of jars of soil collected from sites where Black people were lynched attest to America's violent racist past. Bearing witness to hurt places and to our own ongoing human relationship with them is also the focus of our work with Radical Joy for Hard Times. We encourage people to go in person to places they love that have become damaged or are endangered, places like burnt forests, hurricane-ravaged neighborhoods, landfills, or street corners where an act of violence has occurred. There people share their stories about what the place means to them and spend time walking or sitting quietly in order to get reacquainted with the place as it is now. Finally, they make a gift of beauty for the place. This practice, too, is a way of bearing witness that will become more important as climate change wreaks damage, homelessness, and heartbreak all over the planet. By actually spending time in places that no longer flourish the way they once did and may never do again, and by opening our hearts to our feelings about that new reality, we hone our own boldness.

Attending hurt places can also prepare us to attend hurt people, for hurt places frequently mean hurt people. In 1995 the American Buddhist teacher Bernie Glassman began taking a group to Auschwitz each year to meditate, and the practice has continued after his death in 2018. Participants meditate together at the railroad tracks where Nazi trains stopped to offload millions of people, most of whom would die in that place. Members of the group share their stories—of Jewish ancestors who were killed in the death camps, of German ancestors who contributed to those deaths, of personal sorrows and griefs of many kinds. Prayers and ceremonies, impromptu and planned, arise each day. What people take home is a sense of being rooted in a history that transcends their own family lineage or some impersonal narrative they had learned about in school. They become part of one another's history. Glassman believed that bearing witness at Auschwitz teaches us that we carry inside us all the players in a tragedy: the killers and the killed, the rapist and the raped, the thief and the one who lost his belongings. "After visiting Auschwitz for the first time," Glassman wrote, "I realized that places of great suffering were also places of great healing. But the healing cannot arise until we bear witness to the suffering."[6]

Here is a practice for bearing witness to sorrow without being sucked into it. It is borrowed from the Tibetan Buddhist meditation, *tonglen*. You begin by thinking of a news story about an innocent victim, an injustice, a human-made or natural disaster that has upturned people's lives. Sit quietly as you consider what happened. Track your feelings. Perhaps they are feelings of resistance: you don't want to be here, even mentally, and you long to flee and get on with something more important, like doing the laundry. Stay. Sit. Take in the story with your in-breath. Release it with your out-breath. Do that several times. Now, with the in-breath, imagine that you can absorb some of the sorrow of that person or place. This sorrow does you no harm, it merely expands your capacity for empathy. Then, on the out-breath, send beauty, love, and compassion to the one who is suffering. Do this practice for several minutes. Pema Chödrön describes *tonglen* as "a method for connecting with suffering—our own and that which is all around us, everywhere we go. It is a method of overcoming our fear of suffering and for dissolving the tightness of our hearts. Primarily it is a method for awakening the compassion that is inherent in all of us, no matter how cruel or cold we might seem to be."[7]

27. Go home.

At some point, says existential philosopher Lewis Gordon, you just have to go home. He relates the inner work of going home to becoming a full and authentic human being. For much of your life, he says, you have to expend a lot outward effort to exert your public self, the self you hope will be acknowledged, recognized, befriended. Loved. Sooner or later, however, you must turn in your own direction. You "go home."

Andi Olsen captures the moment when releasing the effort of being public slips over us unawares; Gordon expands and develops that process. He wants "going home" to be deliberate. He wants us to cultivate it. "You can't just stay partying," he told a crowd of students at Southern Illinois University at Edwardsville. "Eventually people have to do something… they've gotta go home. And now you come into this complicated, difficult thing about how you talk about freedom. Home is not simply a place."[1] Home, he continued, is a feeling of comfort in knowing you are in the right situation emotionally and psychologically. As examples, he mentioned choosing a major in college, falling in love, entering into a certain profession and, having made these decisions, nestling into the reality of them and feeling that you have arrived in an inner place that is right for you.

When Jean-Paul Sartre, Simone de Beauvoir, Albert Camus, and the other existentialists of the 1940s and 50s talked about "authenticity," they were, in a sense, talking about "going home." Authenticity, for them, was an antidote to what Sartre called "bad faith," an unexamined willingness to hide our actualized selves behind a preconceived notion of who we are supposed to be, a notion based on what we imagine to be the acceptable things others are doing and expect us to do as well. This revelation came to Sartre one day as he was sitting in his favorite Café de Flore in Paris. He was watching the waiter walk back and forth, emptying his tray, placing glasses on tables, making his way to the kitchen, making his way back. Suddenly it occurred to Sartre that the waiter was engaged not in being a waiter but in playing the part of a waiter. What might his real avocation be? the philosopher asked himself. Maybe he was denying himself a life as an artist, a war hero, a lover. By being authentic, Sartre did not mean getting in touch with an inner, previously neglected "self" and then blossoming under its freshly welcomed aegis. He meant that, from moment to moment, we can make a moral choice about who we are—and claim it. As Gordon would put it, that means "going home."

To go home is to settle into a place that makes your psyche feel safe and comfortable and, at the same time, energized and full of possibilities. It's an emotional place where you take off your coat and hang it in the closet among the other jackets and raincoats that you can choose from when the weather warrants. At home you know where things are. You have a favorite chair. You know where the floor creaks beneath your feet and how long it takes the hot water in the shower to get to the temperature you like. At home you can speak freely. Home, both inner and outer, says Emmanuel Levinas, is a feeling of belonging. Home is the place you go to in order to withdraw from that which is unstable and challenging. It is an interior sanctum of the mind as well as a sanctum in the physical world. In this inner home, Levinas says, "the I recollects dwelling at home with itself". It is a place where you not just *are*, but where you *can*. Where there is an inner freedom to explore, invent, become larger.

However, as Gordon points out and as mainstream conscious-ness has been struggling to grasp in recent years, for many people the possibilities for resting in that authentic home of the self have been repeatedly red-lined. When you broaden the concept of home from the space where you go to sleep at night to the society you live in, Gordon reminds, Black people are not at home in the "home" country where they were born. They are "homeless" in the present because of the circumstances that defined them in the past. They can't relax, because they are being watched, suspected, dismissed, denied. The yearning for home found expression in Gospel and spiritual music, in which "home" means heaven, as in "Go home to my Lord to be free" and "I will try by de grace of God / To win my way home."

In the United States and Europe, white men have been perceived as more entitled than Black, Latinx, indigenous people, and women to live comfortably at home in the world. They can dwell in whatever metaphorical high-rise condos, posh townhouses, and weekend getaways on the shore that they choose. It is assumed that they have a right to do so. The privilege that we white people of both sexes have grown up with and take for granted has blinded most of us to the many ways in which skin color eases or inhibits a person's ability to be at home in the world. As a white woman in my community anti-racist group remarked, "The biggest problem about racism for me was that the subject never came up." A man of indigenous-Mexican heritage reminded us, his colleagues during a board meeting, "I don't have a choice about facing racism. I face it every time I walk out my front door."

Understanding white privilege and how it has influenced those of us who have lived with it without ever having to take stock of all those advantages is a difficult, often painful process, but by sticking with it I can come to recognize my own slanted perspectives and adjust them. I realize with something of a shock how it's far easier for a white person than a person of color to find and contentedly settle in either a physical home in a welcoming neighborhood or a psychological home, where there is space and support for exploring the kinds of interests that lead to friends and opportunities.

Surviving hard times means claiming my right to go home and recognizing the right of others to go to their homes. This is not a process of sitting down to figure out "who I really am" and then, once I've made up my mind, never having to worry about it again. It is a matter of choosing over and over again to act from a place that feels most in alignment with my home-self: what my values are, what I love, what bothers me. For one person "going home" could mean raising an objection when someone makes a racist or sexist joke. For another person claiming that authentic self could be pausing to help a stranger in trouble. Or it could mean stopping to absorb some unexpected beauty, when, for example, a lone violinist playing to the commuting stampede in the Metro station compels you to pause, just for a few seconds, to listen and transcend.

Of course *going home* once doesn't mean *staying* home. We all have to make constant adjustments. A settling-in that feels absolutely right at one time may turn out to be unworkable years or even moments later. We outgrow things, and sometimes we outgrow people or they outgrow us. Circumstances change, often dramatically. We accomplish a goal and, instead of feeling moved to pursue the next logical step on the path, we are compelled to set off in a completely different direction. In my book about the divine Beloved, I explore how that magnetic inner force draws us to pursue certain longings and fascinations that hook us and demand that we give them our full attention. The Beloved lives in all of us, drawing us inexorably to the people, pursuits, and places that some deep, intrinsic part of us knows will be profoundly important, creative, and spiritually rewarding. For me the Beloved showed up to seduce me on a long search to find some way of reconnecting people with the damaged, desecrated places in their midst. The Beloved entices us with the conviction that, by saying Yes to some big, risky, and possibly life-changing prospect, we just might find our true inner home.

During the "sheltering in place" lockdown mandated by the coronavirus pandemic, many people took the opportunity to reflect on what they consider truly important. Having to live with ourselves and with—or without—our families and friends in more restrictive ways, we discovered how restless or content or escapist or pessimistic we were. We had to face our impatience and our gratitude, our longing, and our fear. We asked ourselves how and if, when the world returned to "normal," we would adapt. Would we reclaim the habits and attitudes we'd taken for granted before the world fell ill, or would we find ways to hold on to what we'd discovered that was really valuable, like spending more time with our children or taking day trips in the car instead of flying to faraway vacation destinations? Would we treasure more than ever the friends and family members we had not been able to embrace for so many months? Would we continue to attend to the seasonal changes in our own backyards and neighborhood streets, as we never had before? Would we volunteer for an organization that had touched us when we could only explore it online?

It's impossible to always be at home. Of course, we rarely remain comfortably in this inner "home." As soon as we get what we want, what we think we need, most of us begin itching for something else: a promotion, a new pair of boots, a vacation. Being at home in the moment is the essence of meditation, a practice of being here and now, rather than fretting about the past and worrying about the future, which occupy so much of the time and energy of the human psyche. Yet, as Buddhist writer Mark Epstein points out in his *Advice Not Given*, "The Buddha had the rather paradoxical insight that it is difficult to remain comfortably in the moment because we are afraid of uncertainty and change. The present is not static, after all; it is constantly in motion and we can never be absolutely certain about what the next instant will bring."[2] In meditation, then, we allow our thoughts to rise and dissipate like vapor, as all things must do in life, as we return to the home place of the moment.

To decide that "going home" means to sit around all day in an easy chair watching TV would mean that I fail to accept responsibility for what is mine to do. It would mean I bypass chances to be bigger, bolder, and more creative than I might think I'm capable of being. It would mean that my sense of self, that private soul, becomes isolated and self-involved instead of opening up to the possibilities of the world. But in my challenges, as in my ordinary moments, I can practice "going home." Something is calling me forth right now to a place that is both familiar and new. And, at the same time, I recognize that everyone around me is also trying to "go home" to a place that feels just right and could perhaps use a little encouragement on the journey.

V. GIVE

The most important of all the paths to surviving the sorrows of Earth and self is giving. The other four practices—Sink, Punch, Seek, and Receive—all lead to Give. They help us confront a tough reality and quit deluding ourselves that it's anything other than what it is, while at the same time we refuse to lose ourselves to it. Through the hardest stretches of hard times, those practices sweeten small and surprising moments, reminding us both of the vulnerability and generosity of others and the availability of beauty at any time. Through these simple ways of looking at and responding to our world, we open up to the delight of giving. Giving is the outward gesture that I can—and *must*—take again and again. In the throes of worry, grief, and fear, reaching outward to make an offering to another may seem like the most outrageous suggestion of all. It could be nothing less than martyrdom, pure and simple! A sacrifice only a saint would make!

But offering beauty in hard times, like the other suggestions in this book, does not require denying our own situation or sacrificing priorities of health and well being so that we may fulfill the needs of someone else. It simply means that we are just as open to the impulses to give as we are to the ones to receive. Besides, the kinds of gifts I'm talking about here are not the ones you go out and buy and wrap in pretty paper and ribbon. They are actions. They cost nothing. Usually they require no foresight whatsoever and are given impulsively. Even when we feel that the world has taken from us all that we need and value, it is by giving that we discover that we still do have something to give.

In hard times, many things help, but one absolutely reliable antidote is beauty. Our Radical Joy for Hard Times practice centers on making a gift of beauty for a hurt place, using the materials the place itself provides. The underlying message is that we can make beauty under all kinds of circumstances and also that the ingredients of beauty-making are available everywhere. Nothing extraneous is needed. Beauty found and beauty made break through walls of powerlessness and melt despair. Suddenly there is a shift in how we feel, how we face our world. Suddenly we are not alone, sure that nobody can understand our situation, or that, even if they could, they would not possibly be able help. Finding, and especially making, beauty is like opening a window in a stuffy room. The breeze can't get in unless we open that window. If we only sit and stifle there, complaining and feeling sorry for ourselves, nothing will change. When we make ourselves available to receive beauty, we open that window. When we make beauty for another person or place, we open another window. Then how fragrant and refreshing is that cross-breeze. As the French sociologist and anthropologist Marcel Mauss wrote: "A wise precept has run right through human evolution, and we would be as well to adopt it as a principle of action. We should come out of ourselves and regard the duty of giving as a liberty, for in it there lies no risk."[1]

28. Say goodbye to a glacier.

On August 18, 2019 Iceland officially marked the passing of a national treasure—a glacier. Once, Okjökull had extended its snowy turrets and ice-blue craters across twenty-four square miles. But by 2014 global warming had so dramatically shrunk it that geologists had no choice but to strip it of its status as a glacier. *Jökull* means "glacier" in Icelandic, so now the formerly majestic Okjökull is the meager Ok, bearing no ice mass at all. On that overcast day in August a group of about a hundred people, including Prime Minister Katrín Jakobsdóttir, scientists, artists, dignitaries, activists, and children made a pilgrimage up the mountain to commemorate the demise of the glacier. At a sand-colored rock shaped like half an egg they paused. Jakobsdóttir unveiled a copper plaque affixed to the rock and containing a brief "letter to the future" written by author Andri Snaer Magnason. Under the date of the ceremony and the current atmospheric concentration of carbon dioxide at the site— 415 parts per million, well over the 350 ppm Bill McKibben had urged the world to strive to maintain—the text reads: "In the next 200 years, all our glaciers are expected to follow the same path. This monument is to acknowledge that we know what is happening and what needs to be done. Only you know if we did it."[1] The ceremony, the plaque, the recognition of the need for such an event were signs of the present mourning the actions of its past and holding itself accountable to its future.

Desperate times demand that we ask desperate questions—and attempt through extraordinary actions to answer them. In 1882 when Nietzsche was writing about the death of God, he queried: "How shall we... comfort ourselves?.... What water is there for us to clean ourselves? What festivals of atonement, what sacred games shall we have to invent?"[2] Today, facing the demise of so much that we love of the Earth, we might, in similar vein, ponder, *How can we live with the death of the Earth, especially knowing that we have caused it? What water can we drink that is pure, not laced with chemicals or clotted with invisible pieces of plastic? What festivals, or at least what practices of atonement, of gratitude, of consolation, shall we have to invent?*

It is appropriate and fitting to say goodbye to a loved one through a formal and meaningful action or event, such as a funeral or a memorial service. It also probably makes you feel better. People use the term "closure" so casually, as if an apology from a murderer, the return of the body of a soldier, or the imposition of a steep fine on a corporation responsible for poisoning a river will somehow make suffering people feel so much better that their grief will become smoother and less complicated. But there is no such thing as emotional completion after a great loss, and to expect it and anxiously wait for it just makes us feel that there's something wrong in the world that would be made better if somebody else wasn't withholding the antidote. Even if we get what we want, we're still going to feel sadness and regret.

A ceremony that honors both life and death brings departure and loss into focus, and although you know a funeral is probably going to make you sad—so, prophylactically, you stuff a few sheets of Kleenex into your pocket or purse before leaving home for one— you also trust that it brings people together. We expect to attend funerals or memorial services that mark the passing of friends and family members and feel that something is amiss when that doesn't happen. It's as if the dead person has quietly slipped out of a large and friendly gathering while no one was paying attention and now is wandering around on her own somewhere, lost and perhaps unsafe. A funeral or memorial service enables those who are left behind to call this departed person back into the community for a brief, fixed time in a particular place and offer last expressions of their affection, while also comforting one another. A formal farewell also gives the mourners the courage to touch the monster of death together. Someone was alive, someone had a beautiful quality unlike anyone else's, someone had a unique way of doing this thing or that, a quirk that everyone present can agree on and share a little chuckle about.

And now that person is gone, and through this ceremony the ones remaining are able to say, in effect, *Yes, yes, she is gone and we are here and though we grieve, we must still remain.*

During the coronavirus pandemic, people became very creative in their dedication to the rites of saying goodbye. There were processions of cars, headlights ablaze as in a typical funeral process, but now, instead of stretching in a line down streets, they circled round the block of the deceased, while relatives stood at the windows watching. For one family mourning the death of an elderly matriarch, the distancing restrictions of the virus were particularly painful, as their religious tradition required viewings of an open casket. With the help of their funeral director they found a solution that gave them at least some satisfaction that they were doing things in the right way. The woman lay in her casket in the middle of the church parking lot, while her mourning family paid their respects from a safe distance. When COVID-19 prevented a friend of mine from getting on a plane to attend the burial of her mother, a childhood friend volunteered to share the brief interment ceremony live via Facetime.

As the people in Iceland demonstrated, it is also appropriate and fitting to say goodbye to non-human beloveds. A mountain or bayou or old-growth forest may not have vanished from the Earth, but it can be terribly, uglily changed. When that happens, those who have loved it mourn, because now that mountain or bayou or forest can no longer do what it used to do. The essence of its existence has faded or been amputated. Those who say that the Earth will survive humanity are correct. However, humanity mourns the loss of what it loves, and commemorating that loss is important for the survival of the living. But bidding goodbye to a place doesn't have to entail conscripting a government leader to join you for a long hike or commissioning a brass plaque. It doesn't even have to involve any more than one or two people. It just means being attentive to our own recognition that something we have loved and valued is gone and will not return—and breathing air into that acceptance with an action that expresses our own sorrow about the circumstances. For example, three teenagers in Ithaca, New York have a practice of burying birds, squirrels, snakes, racoons, and other dead animals that they find lying wayside, splayed open or bashed by traffic. If the condition or size of the animal prevents them from burying it, they lay flowers on its body and speak words over it, praising it for its particular running, sniffing, foraging self. "It's a way of saying goodbye to their little life," said sixteen-year-old Safie.

Fran Weinbaum, a wilderness rites of passage guide and goat keeper in Vermont, was distraught that many old trees on her land had to be cut down when she and her husband decided to upgrade their heating system with energy-efficient solar panels. Her distress was aggravated when a technician from the solar company casually dismissed her feelings as "tree trauma." Looking at the cleared land and concrete pads extending over an area that had once been a woodland, she reflected on the sad paradox that the move toward a more sustainable lifestyle had necessitated the destruction of trees that had long predated her oil-burning furnace. "We live in a time of irreconcilable differences, and those realities were now in my own back yard," she wrote. After the cement was poured for the panels, she refused a workman's invitation to press a handprint or a date into the wet pads. By the next morning, however, her sadness had mutated into the first stirrings of acceptance, and she went outside and scratched into the still-damp cement, "Gratitude for trees" and "Gratitude for sun." That expression of thanks segued into a ceremony. She offered prayers and herbs to each of the frost-covered tree stumps. Gradually the new site began to lose its oddity and become part of her home. Fran used the woodchips as mulch for her garden. Her goats munched on the cut boughs. Later she worked with a landscaper to determine what fruit trees, berry bushes, and vines she might plant around the site. Without that simple ceremony of acceptance, she would likely have gotten used to the new site anyway, but with it, she said, she found a sense of balance between destruction and creation, right action and sacrifice.

"Whenever we make changes in our surroundings," writes Tony Hiss in his wonderful book, *The Experience of Place*, "we can all too easily shortchange ourselves by cutting ourselves off from the sights or sounds, the shapes or textures, or other information from a place that have helped mold our understanding and are now necessary for us to thrive."[3] Whenever and wherever the heart feels affection and loss, there is an opportunity to say goodbye in a way that actually brings us closer, not farther away, from that which has left and whose absence saddens us. The physiology of a loved place, moreover, is not restricted to woodlands, glaciers, and animals. Buildings are places too, and narrow country roads and elegant marble archways and all kinds of other things that people admire and feel to be part of their home. When the government of Sydney, Australia announced a plan to tear down Millers Point and other historic public housing buildings on a peninsula jutting out into Sydney Harbor, residents fought the move as "aggressive social cleansing," since the residents who would be displaced were of mixed races and typically earned low incomes. Many people had lived there for decades and worked on the docks close to their homes. Now they were elderly and had nowhere else to go. Protests, lawsuits, and expert testimony failed to save the neighborhood, so one day in June 2019, residents participated in Radical Joy for Hard Times's annual Global Earth Exchange by filling their windows with large signs emblazoned with hearts, writing messages to and about their home and tying them on trees with yellow yarn, and creating hearts on the ground out of pebbles. They could not save their homes or even assure that when they moved, they would remain in close proximity to friends and neighbors, but they could join together to bid goodbye to their home with attention, camaraderie, and beauty. At a point of great helplessness, they could creatively make their mark.

The Radical Joy for Hard Times tribute to wounded places comprises four simple steps that all kinds of people can do for all kinds of places without being experts and without needing tools or equipment or even other people to be effective. Only the first and last of these steps are essential:

- Go to a wounded place.
- Sit awhile and share your stories about what the place means to you.
- Get to know the place as it is now.
- Share what you discovered.
- Make a gift of beauty for the place.

People sometimes want to do this ceremony from their home, without confronting the place directly. They think that by going there they'll feel even more upset about what has happened than they already do. Actually, this first step of facing discomfort and sorrow and getting to know the place anew opens us up in surprising ways. We realize that we are bolder than we thought, that we can face that which we didn't want to face, and that we remain in close relationship with a place, even in its changed state. The next part of the practice, sharing stories of our life with this place, testifies to how important the place has been to each of the people present. Even if it is someone's very first visit to the place, they can still share their first impressions of it and how those correspond to what they knew about the place before arriving. With Step 3, getting to know the place as it is now, we begin to see how the place is struggling to survive, what's growing there, and even how its new life has shaped the community around it. Alone with our own responses, we discover that, even in decline, life goes on, change keeps happening, nothing remains the same. By sharing the tales of what happened in Step 4, what we saw, heard, and felt, we affirm our own ongoing bond with the place and discover how connected our witnessing is to the stories of the others in the group. Hence, the place reveals that its identity, its *personality* is alive and ever-shifting. Step 5 making a gift, is what brings about the radical joy for the tough circumstances of this place. We make the gift out of found materials as a way of reminding ourselves that a gift for a place can be made at any time, without preparation or outside expertise or materials. It also affirms that all places, like all people, have within them the elements they need to be more beautiful.

The flexibility of this ceremony has given it a wide reach among diverse participants. In Bali, members of a village in the northern mountains have woven their own elaborate prayers and ceremonies into RadJoy events, such as the release of a hawk that had been wounded and healed, a tribute to clove trees that had not flowered for two years because excessive rains knocked the blossoms off the branches, and a village cleanup. At Palmer Station in Antarctica, a scientist participated by taking a photograph of her colleague standing in front of a glacier that was shrinking farther and farther away from their scientific research station every year. In North Carolina, two friends made and served grilled cheese sandwiches to everyone who showed up to clean up a littered boat pull-out. The grief that a human being feels for a place they love that has been hurt or endangered is real. Admitting that grief, *evolving mourning* to include nature, homes, and homelands, is vital to making us more compassionate. Creating ceremonies for the place commemorates our love of it and our enduring attachment.

29. Make beauty behavioral.

A one-year-old boy watches a puppet show in which three characters play ball together. The central puppet rolls the ball back and forth to the other two. One of the other puppets, who is helpful and cooperative, rolls the ball back, whereas the third puppet grabs the ball and tries to steal away with it. After the play, the little boy is shown the helpful and the mean puppets. Each holds a treat. The child is told he may choose a treat from either puppet. He takes the treat from the mean puppet—and then he delivers a punishing smack to it.[1] Studies like this, and there have been several, show that even at a very young age children know the difference between naughty and nice. They recognize that sharing is better than keeping, and they have an innate sense of equality and inequality. It seems we humans are hardwired for generosity, fairness, and kindness.

Putting these kinds of attributes into action, whether the actor is a puppet, your spouse, or a corporate policy, is beauty manifested as behavior. When we think of beauty, we tend to think of something that we perceive and appreciatively take in to ourselves, such as a painting, a mountain peak, a face, or a hymn sung by a church choir. But beauty isn't only an outward quality that we receive. It is also a way of acting. It is spiritual egress rather than spiritual entrance. It is a recognition of a dilemma, a hardship, a need somewhere outside of ourselves that we respond to with our body. It is an action motivated by knowledge that there is a gap before us and we are capable of filling it.

If it takes effort to accept that *receiving* beauty can light the dark, it can be tougher still to admit that sowing some beauty of your own into those dark places is good medicine for yourself, as well as others. Suffering can paralyze. Disaster, when it grabs you personally, can upend your ability to think rationally and act sensibly. You get caught in the maelstrom of confusion, grief, and worry and, both to protect yourself from further suffering and protect others from the alarming frenzy you find yourself in, you may shut down even further. Sometimes you act irrationally. Sometimes you lash out. Agitated people can become possessive about their space, their belongings, their very hold on existence, and they distrust "outsiders," whom they accuse of stealing what they feel is theirs or pushing them out of their territory. The presumption of violence on the part of the other can easily lead to an actual act of violence by the accuser, the presumer. Take the example of Kyle Rittenhouse, the teenager who shot and killed two people and wounded another in Kenosha, Wisconsin during protests that followed the 2021 killing of a Black man, Jacob Blake, by a white police officer. Despite evidence in a video (which could not be used in court) showing that Rittenhouse was the first person to aim his gun, the defense team was successful in getting him acquitted because he claimed he was only defending himself. The jury believed that Rittenhouse's presumption of violence justified his actual violence.

Yet if calamity often stuns the senses and (literally) triggers outbursts, it can also compel us to reach out with kindness. In the spring of 2019, for example, a young Kansas woman purchased every last pair of shoes from a local PayLess store that was going out of business and donated them to people in Nebraska who had lost their homes and farms to massive flooding. When Hurricane Harvey left many Houstonians homeless, a man who owned a chain of mattress stores turned his showrooms into shelters for those needing a place to stay. In such instances, the plight of others overshadowed the givers' preoccupation with their own plights, enabling them to respond with extreme acts of beautiful behavior. The impulse to give simply because doing so seems absolutely necessary at the moment, is what's crucial in behavioral beauty. During one of his daily news broadcasts during the early weeks of the coronavirus pandemic, when New York City was Ground Zero of cases, New York Governor Andrew Cuomo read aloud a letter he had received from a retired farmer in Kansas. The man wrote that he and his wife were both in their seventies, and she had only one lung. "Frankly, I am afraid for her," he wrote. "Enclosed, find a solitary N95 mask left over from my farming days. It has never been used. If you could, would you please give this mask to a nurse or doctor in your city? I have kept four masks for my immediate family."[2] What was one mask in a city groaning under the weight of COVID? It was monumental. It was medicine. It may have gone onto the face of one person, but it went into the hearts of millions.

In the thick of emergency, it is the stuff of survival that people need: food, water, their prescriptions, warm clothes, a place to sleep. As the crisis itself begins to fade and survivors start to patch together the components of a new life, acts of beauty can have a profound impact. In December of 2017, Tricia Woods and her family returned to what had been their front lawn in the Coffey Park section of Santa Rosa, California before the entire community was consumed by wildfire. Now the house was gone, and even the ash of family photos, children's drawings, good china, and laptops had been carted away to the landfill. The ground was bare and charred. The reason the family had come that day to their former home, however, was not to mourn but to put up a Christmas tree. They decorated it and encircled it with twinkling battery-powered lights. When their former neighbors heard about the tree and went to see it, they recognized it as a beacon of stubborn determination to prevail. They began bringing Christmas trees of their own to the neighborhood. Some added fanciful touches, such as a sign leaning against a charred mailbox directing Santa Claus to the family's temporary address. A twelve-year-old girl did a dance around the tree she and her family trimmed. Newspapers and TV stations covered the story, and many people came to visit.

We depend on stories of courage and self-sacrifice like these, not only because they tell us that there is relief and even delight in hard times, but also because they imbue us with a spark of belief that we, too, will have the courage to bestow acts of beauty when others are suffering. In fact, Jean Case, writing in *Forbes* magazine, believes that a tendency to offer compassion and generosity in emergency situations is a sign that Americans will behave charitably as global warming mounts. Stories of super-kindness demonstrate that people aren't as divided as we think, she wrote, that, in fact, we are very inventive, and that both the public and private sectors will respond in times of trouble.[3]

Behavioral beauty has been shown to shift feelings and motivate actions in givers and receivers alike. A 2008 study by Michael Norton and his colleagues at Harvard Business School found that of all the people who received bonuses at a Boston-based company, those who reported that they had spent their money on others were happier than those who had spent it on themselves.[4] Beautiful acts also tend to stimulate further beautiful acts, as the first Christmas tree in charred Coffey Park inspired a festive illumination of the whole neighborhood. In fact, empathy—and by extension the actions that arise from it—turns out not to be a fixed trait that one is born with, but is actually more like a muscle that we can strengthen with practice. In his 2016 study Stanford University psychologist Jamal Zaki and his team gave participants a $1.00 "bonus" in addition to the fee they got for completing the study. They asked the participants to look over a list of charitable organizations and decide if they would like to contribute to any of them. Those who believed that other people had contributed generously tended to make higher donations themselves. "We find that people imitate not only the particulars of positive actions, but also the spirit underlying them," Zaki said. "This implies that kindness itself is contagious, and that it can cascade across people, taking on new forms along the way."[5] A little child attests to this principle when he recognizes the niceness of one puppet and rebukes another for its selfishness.

Making beauty behavioral also means letting people know what I see and appreciate about them. I might note, for example, the way a friend pauses in the middle of a conversation to turn all his attention to his child. Do I tell him that I admire this characteristic of his? If I find myself seized by appreciation for a young woman wearing a colorful cloth mask over her face as she carefully arranges cans of soup on a supermarket shelf during the early weeks of Covid, do I express my thoughts in words or keep them to myself? Praise is an antidote to grief, because it reverses the heavy burden of self that I am lugging around. It pitches beauty outward at a time when I'm tempted to believe that I'm entitled to receive a lot and am exempt from giving. It shows me that, indeed, I truly am capable of more. You let a friend know how much you appreciate her. You sneak up on your loved one and give him a kiss. You help a stranger struggling with a heavy bag. The literary deconstructionist Jacques Derrida described the best gifts as "the extraordinary, the unusual, the strange, the extravagant, the absurd, the mad."[6]

Beauty can even be a start to reconciliation. In an article in the *New York Times Magazine*, Ojibwe David Treuer describes a ceremony that united two tribes with a sad and tangled history. In 1750 an Ojibwe war party had attacked a Dakota village, slaughtering every woman, man, and child they encountered and pouring powder down the smokeholes of the lodges, burning alive everyone who was inside. For about a hundred years the two tribes lived in wary proximity. Then, one day, a band of Dakota showed up at the Ojibwe Mille Lacs reservation with a gift, a big drum. They asked every Ojibwe who had "touched blood," or killed a Dakota person in close contact, to take a seat. These were their places of self-acknowledgment, of taking responsibility for what they had done. The gift givers explained that, as the years passed and the ceremony spread to other communities, eventually no one would be alive who had killed a Dakota. Then the seats could be occupied by those who had killed someone else. Eventually, there would be no one left who had taken the life of another. The Big Drum that the Dakota presented to their enemy has long since been succeeded by other Big Drums, "made out of ... barrels cut in half with a raw hide stretched over the open ends, painted, decorated. It is also a ceremony (made up mostly of singing, talking, eating and dancing), and it is a society (made up of people from the community in which the drum sits)."[7]

Imagine how powerful a ceremony like this would be if white

people, descendants of colonizers and slave owners, were to accept an invitation from Native American, Black, and other people of color to occupy seats of culpability in their communities. We would acknowledge the ways that we have been complicit, no matter how much in innocence or ignorance, of taking advantage of our white privilege. They would be ceremonies not of blame but of facing those who have been wronged and accepting responsibility.

Behavioral beauty is a gift that requires neither money nor expertise. A tale from twelfth-century France tells of a man who spent his young years working as a tumbler and acrobat at village fairs. When he gets older, he joins the monastery of Clairvaux and eventually becomes a monk himself. However, he always feels inferior to the other monks, because he doesn't have the skills that they have. He isn't educated. He can't join in prayer and songs because he doesn't know how read. One day, alone in the chapel, he stands before the statue of the Virgin Mary and offers the only gift he's capable of: he does his acrobatics for her. He is much older now and doesn't have the dexterity he once had, but he puts his whole heart into it. One of the other monks spies him and brings the abbot to witness the scene. But as they watch, they see the man fall into a faint from all his exertion, and then the Virgin Mary steps down from her pedestal and wipes his face.

This story is moving, because it points out that beautiful behavior can take all kinds of forms. We imagine that the observing monk and the abbot might have been prepared to chastise the acrobatic monk for his outrageous, possibly sacrilegious act. The Virgin Mary saw it differently. Beautiful behavior might not look the way we expect it to. Shortly after Radical Joy for Hard Times was founded and we were looking for a symbol or image to express our conviction that radical joy can be found and created in many ways for hurt places, we used a photograph of a woman doing a cartwheel in a clearcut forest. Some people, including the writer Derrick Jensen, were upset by this image. They thought it insensitive, disrespectful: *How could anyone act foolish and playful in the face of such depredation?* But the image, and the action, were meant as a way of saying: *I am dedicated to bringing my offering to this wounded place in as life-affirming and creative a way as possible. Along with my sorrow, therefore, I bring my mad, outrageous, bold gift of play, levity, and full-bodied charity.*

Survival and what I call "thrival" depends both on working for change in the future and taking right action in the present. On one level, your entire body and your mind, as best as it's able, are taking in the total picture of your situation at every minute. Sometimes you're in the midst of a desperate situation, and you can't pretend otherwise. Understandably, you want things to be different and, depending upon what kind of person you are, you may try to bring that difference into form through protest, volunteering, prayer, art, or counseling, Or you may go to a movie to try and forget it all. At the same time, embedded in each and every moment of the larger reality, like seeds in the ground of a vast field, are opportunities to express those extraordinary, unusual, and mad gifts Derrida championed. Rather than enacting beauty as a way to forget a hard predicament, we do so to acknowledge that predicament and the deep affect it has on our lives, even as we remind ourselves that we wield some power over it. We make beauty in the moment in order to bear up for an hour or a day.

Beauty won't save the Earth, of course. Action is crucial and must include legislative, artistic, medical, educational, judicial, agricultural, spiritual, and many other kinds of responses. The making of beauty, however, can be part of any other branch of redress for the Earth's great problems. We must make our communities as lovely and welcoming as possible, even when they are faltering under the assaults of climate change and other ecological challenges. A friend from Haiti told me that, even in the poorest neighborhoods, people plant flowers in coffee cans and old buckets and place them in front of their homes. We must offer funeral ceremonies for decapitated mountains, the sick soil of brownfields, and vanishing bats and honeybees. We must teach our children to raise their eyes from the glowing screens of their devices into the night sky and gasp with wonder at the few pale stars that pierce the bleached canopy of city lights. Instead of avoiding clearcut forests, we must visit them and reflect on the decades of their growth and the mere seconds of our use of the products for which they've been sacrificed. We must develop active compassion and beautiful acts for people who are suffering, even when those people adhere to religious or political beliefs different from our own. We must take time within the framework of our passionate activism to share the stories of what a river or canyon or historic neighborhood means to those of us who are working so hard to save it. We must appreciate one another whenever we can, not just inwardly but with words. And we must create behavioral beauty every day, no matter where we are.

30. Donate patience.

For more than a year after my husband died a minor problem with my printer or a long wait on hold would send me into a helpless rage, and I would scream and swear so loudly that my throat hurt for hours. If I was waiting at a stop sign behind at a driver who, in my opinion, was taking an inordinately long time to look back and forth, back and forth, as if waiting for a car to appear that would make it worth stopping for, I would scream at them from the safehouse of my closed car. Once, a sudden and inexplicable Microsoft Word phenomenon interrupted my writing and in my outrage, I swept a stack of papers off my desk. In those moments of furious impatience I felt like my blood was boiling and my agitated cells might jump right out of my skin. It turns out, I wasn't far wrong. Something really is happening in the body when anxiety overtakes us.

Studies have shown that in times of stress, the actual physiology of the brain changes. Ordinarily, the prefrontal cortex, located behind the forehead and responsible for planning, rational thought, and problem solving, works well with the anterior cingulate cortex, which is deeper in the brain and modulates strong emotions. Even deeper in the skull is the amygdala, sometimes called "the fear center." Its job is to scope out our environment and pounce on anything that might be a threat, so it can warn us away from it. If the three functions are in sync, as they normally are, they steady us and prevent us from reacting in harmful ways when our emotions are on edge. If they're not, we do things we later regret, like cutting too close to a car whose highway behavior has affronted us. In a traumatized person the whole tripartite system goes out of whack. The prefrontal cortex and the anterior cingulate cortex become underactive, while the fear response amps up.[1] Coping gets even harder as those physiological reactions dominate. We become disoriented and edgy. The intensity and urgency of what we must deal with seem so immense that anything else in the world, including people, that aren't immediately relatable to our own distress and its possible relief can look like mere annoyances that must be tolerated or even punished. Tempers flare, especially when the emergency situation keeps demanding our attention and effort as we stand in long lines, fill out endless forms, or wait on hold while cheery canned voices thank us for our patience and tell us how important our business is.

During the years of the COVID-19 pandemic, millions of anxious, scared, and angry people became a safety threat once they got into their cars. Traffic accidents increased dramatically, and in the first half of 2021, the National Highway Traffic Safety Administration reported the biggest six-month jump in traffic deaths ever recorded, with twenty thousand pedestrians, bike riders, and drivers dying in vehicular accidents.[2] Cars offered a means of tearing out of the intolerable stuckness of lockdown and the frustrations of shuttered restaurants, shops, and movie theaters, unpredictable work requirements, and tensions within the family, with everyone forced to cram work, school, meals, play, and sleep into the same home space. So people tried to outrun their stress by escaping in their cars, and sometimes the result was the end of a life, their own or that of another.

In cases of extreme stress, we become lost in the strange precinct that used to be our own familiar world, unable to make decisions or set priorities. A woman whose little beachside home on the Florida coast was destroyed by Hurricane Irma in 2017 told me that she and her friends referred to the mental condition they found themselves suffering as "Hurricane Brain." In those weeks after the storm, she would walk into a grocery store only to discover that she had no idea what to buy. Every time she returned to the site of her house, she would pick through the scattered debris without any sense of what was worth saving and what she ought to start thinking of as waste. The immense loss that she and her community had sustained robbed her not only of her physical home but her emotional center as well.

It took several weeks before she began to feel that her body and brain were aligned and functioning in her behalf.

Amit Sood, a doctor at Mayo Clinic who has studied the physical effects of impatience, told a reporter that the opposite of patience isn't just impatience, it's "anxiety, illness, addiction, loneliness, and death." Impatience even erodes our DNA. Capping the end of each X-shaped chromosome in our body is a small structure called a telomere. The telomeres protect the chromosome from damage and assure that cells get replicated correctly when they divide. As we age, the telomeres get shorter. However, they can also shorten because of certain lifestyle habits, like smoking, lack of exercise, poor diet— and stress. "An episode of explosive anger, stress, or impatience can increase your risk of heart attack and sudden death by two to eightfold for the next few hours," said Sood. Every outbreak of impatience, in other words, ages you.[3]

But telling ourselves that we must "try to be more patient" just sounds like another provocation to stress. It's like the impossible charge that beginning meditators sometimes set themselves: "trying to make my mind blank." It doesn't work. Trying requires effort, and the exertion of effort in difficult times can cause more anxiety and impatience. For me the practice of "donating" patience works much better. When I'm waiting behind a frustratingly cautious driver at a stop sign and notice that my blood is heating up, I can reverse the effects by donating some patience—to the street, the driver, other people passing by, trees and birds—and my cells. It's easy to give a little bit of patience, like simply breathing out, particularly when I think of how it's benefiting my telomeres Choosing patience has just as direct an influence on our physiology as succumbing to stress.

An Oneida tale reminds us of the value of patience—and also attests to the fact that people have long confronted the problematic results of impatience. It seems a turtle noticed the birds flying south for the winter, where the weather was warm and there was lots of good food. He was envious and begged repeatedly to be taken along until finally the birds agreed. They told him that two of them would carry the ends of a stick in their beaks, and the turtle could hitch a ride by biting on the middle of the stick. "But you mustn't open your mouth!" they warned. They all set out, a flock of birds and one turtle with an unrealistic plan. Before long, the turtle got impatient. He tried wriggling his legs to get the birds' attention, but they were too busy flying to notice. So he opened his mouth to ask, "Are we there yet?" The birds didn't hear, because by that time the turtle was falling back to Earth. That's why the turtle hides out in his shell.

31. Get dirty.

Children love to get dirty. They splash about in mud puddles, slither their hands around their finger paintings, and enthusiastically smear gooey chocolate birthday cake all over their hands and mouths. When they get dirty, they're indulging in their environment without restraint, getting intimate with it. Eating it. We reject that kind of intimacy with the unclean as we grow up. After all, who wants to touch something that's been who-knows-where and handled by who-knows-whom? When Sen. Amy Klobuchar, lacking utensils, ate a salad with her comb on a short flight during her 2020 run for president and then ordered an aide to clean the comb, the image of putting into one's mouth a probably oily, possibly dandruffy object that had been lying around in a purse was so gross that it led to countless jokes, opened up a flood of reports about Klobuchar's tyrannical attitude toward her staff, and hurt her credibility as a candidate. Being in contact with something dirty makes you feel that more than just your skin is being soiled. Something internal, something having to do with your safety and sense of self-preservation gets begrimed as well when the dirt of the world gets too close. However, getting dirty can offer valuable lessons in what's really important to survival.

The Finnish philosopher Olli Lagerspetz points out that dirt is not a scientific concept but a cultural one, learned and universal. Every society has some idea of what is clean and what is dirty, and the physically dirty is often associated with the spiritually or morally impure. Messing about with what your society perceives as filth means tainting yourself with abjection and lowliness, especially when it encroaches on something the culture holds in high esteem, something presumed to be immune from dirt. Would people have become so incensed over Andres Serrano's sculpture "Piss Christ," Lagerspetz asks, if the artist had not dared to place the crucifix in a jar of his own urine, juxtaposing the sacred and the profane? When we think of dirt, we don't think of it in the abstract, as a separate thing. We think about it in terms of human involvement. Something is dirty when it contaminates the clean. A thing or person that gets dirty is automatically assumed to be a candidate for cleaning. We clean up our houses when we're expecting company. We take out the trash. We shut the door when we go to the toilet.

We avoid dirt and we especially avoid being considered dirty. So why would anyone *choose* to get dirty? The kind of getting dirty I'm talking about here isn't putting your hands in the soil with gardening. Soil is only dirty when it's smeared on something that you want kept clean, not when it's underneath your fingernails after a happy morning planting flowers. I'm talking about being uncomfortable and rubbing up against situations that haven't seen any soap and water for a while. Many millions of us are going to get irreparably dirty as climate change heaves our homes and belongings around and forces us to adapt and adjust and put up with misery in a way that many of us probably thought we were immune to. Practicing being dirty before that happens is a solid way to prepare and perhaps garner some grace and compassion in the process.

For Roshi Bernie Glassman "street retreats" were a spiritual practice aimed at giving participants an experience of the way many people are forced to exist. For five days members of his metropolitan sangha lived as homeless people in a large city such as New York, San Francisco, or Zurich. They carried no money, jewelry, credit cards, or change of clothes, and they abstained from any actions or easy fixes that would alleviate discomfort. If they were hungry, they had to beg for food or the money to buy something to eat. They had to find what toilets they could, which often entailed the humiliation of being chased out of the ones they managed to enter. At night they had to scavenge for cardboard, plastic, or other materials with which to make a bed. It was a lesson in having little and getting comfortable with both how to provide for basic needs and how to receive help from others. Glassman describes one woman who was at first squeamish about sleeping on dirty, cast-off materials left in dumpsters and on street corners. After one night without them, however, she began riffling determinedly through trash heaps she had previously shunned. Many of the participants in these street retreats said that their friends and family were appalled when they learned about their loved one's plans. However, wrote Glassman, most people, "[w]hether they're corporate executives or busy professionals... say they feel freer on the streets at a street retreat than they've felt for years.... On the streets, with no money or credit cards in their pockets, just the clothes on their backs, they're happy." [1] The street retreat showed people their own resourcefulness, made them look anew at all the possessions in their lives that they valued so much, and gave them compassion for people who were living from hour to hour not because it was a path toward spirituality but because they had no other choice.

There are many ways to get a little dirtier than we're comfortable with. Maybe you volunteer to pick up litter for the national Adopt-a-Highway program. Andy and I did that for years on a two-mile stretch of country road in front of our house, and some of what we gingerly dropped into our trash bags was truly disgusting: balled-up baby diapers, soiled underpants, a McDonald's bag filled with rotting food. Like the woman on the street retreat who didn't want to scavenge for cast-off sleeping materials, some people react to that which has been too long on the street, including human beings, as fouled. Volunteering to help out in a soup kitchen or pausing to have a conversation with a person who is homeless and begging for money would be one way to overcome that kind of queasiness. Entrepreneurs in the California Bay Area, Houston, and Los Angeles offer "toxic tours" in communities where the dominant landmarks are incinerators, petrochemical plants, or brownfields. Clients meet with members of the community and listen to personal stories of their struggles with sickness in their families and indifference on the parts of the government and the industry responsible for the pollution.

Getting dirty might be mental rather than physical. We can get dirty when we catch ourselves distancing from an act of injustice and instead step forth and speak out. Remaining uninvolved can be a way to evade messiness and preserve our treasured personal pristineness. Taking on a new and stickier intimacy with what I wish to avoid could also mean sitting down to have an honest discussion with a friend or family member about something that has gone awry in a once solid relationship. This conversation would not be about convincing the other of the rightness of my personal view, or allowing them to convince me. It's not about "cleaning" anybody up. The point is to air the dirty linen, so we can learn about the emotional burdens each of us has been bearing and rediscover the things that matter to us both. Such actions are often difficult, since they highlight my insecurities, my mistakes, my secret needs and expectations, and especially my vulnerability. However, they can result in substantial healing if everyone involved is willing to be honest. For many white people like me, getting dirty has come to mean entering into awkward conversations about racial privilege and how we have benefited in ways we took for granted. Accepting where and how I have gone awry, how I have overlooked the life reality of another can make me feel foolish, naïve, and ashamed. But in order to adjust my thinking and my behavior, I have to endure the discomfort in order to let new information in to my consciousness and then use it to adjust my attitudes. Getting dirty is almost always about agreeing to get uncomfortable.

My organization, Radical Joy for Hard Times, is dedicated to finding and making beauty in wounded places. Our practice entails going out and getting dirty by confronting places that have become almost taboo by virtue of their devolution into dirtiness, brokenness, pollution, or neglect. These sites are everywhere. No region on Earth avoids them, though the people who live nearby often try to do so. When we go to these places, we settle into what has happened there and pay attention to how the place is responding, for places, like people, are always in flux, always responding heartily to the changing conditions into which they are plunged. Becoming re-engaged with the physical reality of a hazardous waste site or a playground in the shadow of a natural gas processing facility, we recognize anew our bond with the Earth and all who live upon it. Something strange happens when people go to these wounded places. They realize that the beauty they discover there shimmers forth not despite the brokenness, but because of it. They see how nature thrives and how people, out of necessity and love and pure stubbornness, thrive in the midst of nature as it deals with all kinds of challenging circumstances. People pushing through, nature pushing through—it touches a part of us that we never expected to be touched in the midst of such an excursion. To rise out of the muck, to see how the muck is part of life, and to do this by taking the time to get acquainted with the muck is a great feat. It stuns and moves us, whether the dirty, amazing thing is a river, a tree, a person, or our very own self.

During the coronavirus pandemic, the concept of "getting dirty" took on an entirely new meaning. Although the world around us looked the same, it was suddenly very different and very threatening. The flowers bloomed, then the leaves fell from the trees, then the snow drifted down. Yet in those long months, especially before the vaccines were released, we became loath to touch objects that could have been handled even briefly by someone we didn't know. The very air we breathed became potentially lethal, so we wore masks to protect ourselves from the breaths of others. We learned to keep at least six feet of distance between ourselves and strangers. And we gained a new appreciation for those whose livelihoods depended on daily confronting and administering to those who were or could be infected, people like nurses and doctors, supermarket employees, and those who delivered take-out food to the houses of strangers. Many of the people who took those risks and did those jobs got sick themselves. The familiar world became dangerously infected, and our attitudes suffered as well. My stepdaughter told me how baffled her three-year-old son was when, all of a sudden, he was not allowed to run over to other children in the park and start playing with them.

We need to bear witness in person. We need to be willing to face some unpleasantness, something we fear might upset us, might dirty our thoughts or our bodies or both. The willingness to have my outlook smudged helps me discover that I can find familiarity and compassion and even a new sense of "home" in the murky and unfamiliar. By agreeing to get dirty now and then, I become more courageous. I can sit through the bad times in my life and even sink into the yucky, sticky suction of them knowing that my inner being is not contaminated there but is, in fact, being enlightened, cleansed, and expanded.

32. Volunteer for Earth Hospice.

What we consume is now consuming us. Chris Jordan's powerful photographs reveal the amalgam of plastic waste in the bellies of baby albatrosses. Even baby humans have now become carriers of the trash of the Earth. Scientists have traced more than two hundred chemicals in the umbilical cord of a newborn child.[1] The world is not what it seems. Beneath many of its seemingly benign surfaces it is laced and smeared and awash with poison. Recent studies show that almost all the drinking water on Earth, including 93% of bottled water, contains microplastics, tiny particles that break off from clothing, cosmetics, fishing nets, and the gradual dissolving of larger items through the action of sun and waves. Plastic drifts in the blood, lodges in the stomach, sticks to the throat. Human, animal, bird, fish, river, sea, soil, or wind—you can't escape it. The manufacture, use, and disposal of plastic have even forged a new kind of rock, dubbed "plastiglomerate." These coagulated clumps contain rock, sand, and shells, all glued together by plastic waste that was burned by humans who wanted to get rid of it after they'd used it once.

Nature as we have known it is vanishing. The seasons are out of balance. Invasive species are taking over the habitats of natives, who are killed outright or flee because they can't compete with the aggressive new competition. Between 2001 and 2014, one hundred and seventy-three species vanished forever, and recent studies show that in the next fifty years one-third of all the living animal and plant species on Earth may disappear forever.[2] Hotter oceans and hotter air clash to incite extreme weather that destroys homes, rearranges coastlines, heaves water into land and land into water, and leaves people homeless. Farmers struggle to adapt. Young people are terrified. We cannot escape. We cannot "solve the climate crisis" or "turn back global warming." The mediocre efforts that humans and governments propose at their summits, pronounced almost with a wink to show they don't really mean it, are far from our best efforts, and at this stage even our best efforts would be to no avail. We cannot pull our planet back from the course it's on. The ravages of climate change are likely to last decades, even centuries. What will we do, then, to live with the ending of life in our world as we have loved and relied on it?

We need to volunteer for Earth hospice. We must not only acknowledge the loss of the world we love, we must also care for it *and for ourselves* as we undergo that process of losing. This, obviously, is not an easy task, nor a pleasant one. But it will be a very necessary one as we figure out how to do it together. It can also be a meaningful and sacred avocation.

Hospice is a practice, a presence, a place, and a span of time. It is a portal we step through when we finally quit denying that a life as we have known it is ending, and we begin saying goodbye. Hospice differs from active medical care in that it is largely non-interventional. Whereas the dying person in hospice may receive drugs to alleviate pain, extreme measures such as feeding tubes, CPR, and other forms of life support cease. Hospice is a centrifugal winding-down for the dying person—and for their loved ones. It does not entail fixing anything, wrote hospice physician Steven Levine, or even saying the right thing. "As long as we are thinking of healing as opposed to dying, there will be confusion. As long as we separate life from death, we separate the mind from the heart and we will always have something to protect, something more to be, another cause for inharmony and illness. When the attitude toward healing is in balance, the attitude toward death is as well."[3] Hospice insists, *Even though nothing can be done to improve the situation, the situation as it is can be eased.*

My husband Andy went into hospice two and a half days before he died. There were only eight or ten rooms for patients, and the entire place was decorated less like the clinic I had anticipated than a small hotel, with paintings on the walls and comfortable chairs in the hallway, where family members could sit while medical workers were attending the dying person in their room. Andy had a quiet corner room that I had picked out for him, with woods in the back and a garden on the side. There was a bed for me to sleep in and a private bathroom. I was able to sit with him and hold his hand, stroke his cheek, and talk with him in the brief moments when he emerged from the long, private trek he was on. On the first day he entered, he was still conscious. On the second day, he plunged more deeply into a dream world from which he only occasionally emerged. That afternoon he slipped into unconsciousness, and on the night of the third day he died.

I was very calm and present at this vigil. I felt no fear, and my grief was different from the stabbing pain that would start wracking me the following day after I returned alone to our home. During that time in the hospice, my grief was more like a great pool of golden light that I floated in, holding my beloved gently until that moment when he would no longer need any support from me. I wept, but I also did ceremony for him, talked to him, told him I loved him, and assured him that he could go when he was ready. I also tended myself by talking to my friends on the phone, cooking simple meals in the hospice kitchen, and doing crossword puzzles. It wasn't until months later that I realized that my whole focus had been to make Andy's transition as easy and smooth as possible.

Hospice is a time of tears, touch, sorrow, gratitude, waiting, weeping, touching, and loving. Especially loving. For the dying person it is the final journey, accepted and, as much as possible, welcomed. For loved ones, it is bearing witness to the great mystery of death. The average stay in a hospice is two days. Earth hospice will be a longer process. Species of birds and frogs and elephants don't crash to a halt in a few days; that process takes decades. Rivers will die more quickly, as will coastlines. In his book *Collapse*, Jared Diamond ponders the once-verdant island of Rapa Nui, Easter Island, which received its first settlers, migrants from Polynesia, around the year 1200. Over the next few centuries the islanders used the abundant palm trees of their land in many ways: for firewood, making canoes, and constructing conveyances to transport the gigantic sculptures of stone heads for which the place has become famous. The forest thinned year by year by year, and eventually there would have been only one palm tree standing. Diamond wonders: "What did the Easter Islander who cut down the last palm say while he was doing it?"[4] Like the Easter Islanders who may not have noticed when a forest became a small crop, which became a single tree, we won't notice when many of the loved beings and places around us have vanished. But as we witness the process of their decline, the least we can do is offer something back to them. Ash trees, lakes, warblers, and foxes are inextricably woven into the fabric of our lives. Often they comfort us when we are sad, worried, or confused. Now it is our turn to be with them in their final days. This is not a practice of anthropomorphism. We will not attribute feelings of grief to forests and frogs. It is simply recognition of the inherent beauty and dignity of the natural world and its profound influence on our lives. When we do Earth hospice work, we open up to the enormity of life, beauty, decline, and death.

Citing the work of Radical Joy for Hard Times in her article, "Environmental Hospice and Memorial as Redemption: Public Rituals for Renewal," in the *Western Journal of Communication,* Jennifer L. Adams points out that, like human hospice, Earth hospice is not only for the patient but for the survivors as well. It is a process, she argues, that entails "mediating the physical pain of death through palliative care and the emotional feelings of loss through psychological counseling and talk therapy…. [I]t must also offer bereavement support to help family, partners and close friends deal with both anticipatory grief and traditional post-loss grief for at least a year after the death." It is a process of providing the one who is dying and their loved ones a refuge of honesty, compassion, and comfort."[5]

The Earth, of course, is a living planet that has been burning, flooding, tilting, freezing and thawing for four and a half billion years and even now, with the horror of climate change, it is not really dying. What is dying, however, is the Earth that we and our ancestors have known and loved and felt reverence for. Entering into the practice of Earth hospice means bringing the same attitude of patience, kindness, love, and honesty to the situation, while adjusting the practices of human hospice. It means sitting with hurt or endangered places, knowing that I can't save them, but also that I don't have to abandon them. Just the opposite: I can abide by them and open my heart to them.

I believe that my practice of holding vigils in hurt places prepared me for accompanying Andy on his last journey. My very first hospice vigil had occurred many years earlier. It was for a maple tree in Brooklyn, New York. Although I was not so calm and patient then as I was in Andy's final days, I did intuit what had to be done and did it. On an October afternoon I had been rushing to finish a deadline and get to a meeting in Manhattan when my attention was sliced clean through by a loud, grinding noise coming from the back of our apartment house. Because I had lived in New York City for more than twenty years, I had a typical New Yorker's attitude to interruptions: *Loud things are always starting and stopping, and they probably have nothing to do with me.* So, at first, I ignored the noise. After a few minutes, however, it became clear that not only was it not going away, it was also very close. I got up and walked through the apartment to the dining room at the back. The windows looked out on the back yards that stretched behind the brownstones on our block and those on the next block over. In the yard just behind our landlord's garden stood an enormous maple tree. Which now was under siege by men with chainsaws. One man, secured by a harness, straddled a branch about two-thirds of the way up to the top. That morning the branch had been immersed in foliage. Now it was a long bare pole. Another man stood on the ground, hauling away timber that had already been hacked. They were cutting the tree down.

I loved that tree. Probably at least eighty years old, it was so broad and full that it blocked the view of three or four brownstones and yards behind it. In summer it was a vibrating, expansive globe of green. It was an avian Julliard School, with all the musicians practicing at once. In storms, the maple got wild. The branches swayed with the wind, revealing the lights of the Brooklyn Academy of Music a mile away. In all seasons squirrels would leap acrobatically along its woody roads. During thunderstorms, flashes of lightning illuminated the whipping branches and silvered the frenetic leaves. In snow, its bare branches were an etching that stretched across the backyards of Brooklyn.

As if delimbed myself, I sank down onto the floor by the window. And for the next two hours I ministered to the death of that tree. I saw the twigs hacked off to bare the branches. I saw the autumn leaves tremble as the saw sliced through the wood before cutting it through. I watched the branches drop, one at a time. I saw the houses on the other side of the yard being slowly revealed. I just crouched there by the window, watching and weeping. I didn't want to be there. I wanted to get up off the floor, back away from that window, and leave. I wanted to get back to work or get on the subway and go into Manhattan, read a book, get a cup of coffee, do anything to forget all this. But I felt I could not abandon the tree. I had to sit with it, make sure it didn't die alone, and remember its life as that life was being eradicated. To leave the tree during its travail would have seemed an act of betrayal. *Your suffering is witnessed. I voluntarily take on some of what you experience. In whatever way I can, I share it with you. I love you. I will not abandon you.*

Since then I have sat with clearcut forests, gas fracking sites, quarries gouged into the Earth, littered beaches, and a site of war and violence on the border between Palestine and Jordan. The work of Radical Joy for Hard Times is to sit vigil with the places we love and give them beauty, while opening up to the gratitude and grief of our relationship with them. Places are inextricably woven into the fabric of our lives. The least we can do is offer something back to them when they are under duress. This attitude is not anthropomorphism but simply recognition of the inherent beauty and dignity of the natural world and its profound influence on our lives.

People in the western world already have practice with saying goodbye to that which they are attached to but not personally related to. Acts of violence like the destruction of the World Trade Towers on September 11, the death of Princess Diana, and the bombing of a concert in Paris often move people to create impromptu memorials by placing flowers, notes, Teddy bears, candles, and cards at the site of the disaster or some other meaningful public place. They tend these markers of remembrance, freshening the flowers, picking up litter, and falling into conversations with strangers with whom they suddenly have grief in common. Andy and I spent a few weeks in Paris in 2016 shortly after the terrorist bombing there. The central monument in the Place de la République was completely encircled with flowers, hearts, notes, and candles. Wishing to contribute a symbolic act of shared sorrow, I used leaves to make a RadJoy Bird on the ground, while Andy did Tai Chi in memory of those who had lost their lives.

We need now to construct memorials on behalf of those who are still here among us but whose existence is noticeably curtailed. That means we must be prepared to volunteer for Earth Hospice. We can start small: sit with an ash tree that's infested with the emerald ash borer, or pause to bear witness when we drive by a farm dotted with the white, cramped boxes where young calves are condemned to spend their short lives being fattened up to become veal. Make a cairn for vanishing bird species, playing a recording of their songs as we place each stone. Offer a ceremonial gift of water to a diminishing lake or river. The next time you hear statistics about extinction, instead of ignoring the vise of fear and sorrow that grips your gut, move away from the computer for a minute or put down the newspaper and simply take in the bundled knot of love and grief you feel. Touch trees when you pass them, bow to the creek, look at the sky throughout the day and notice what it's doing. Be present. By practicing Earth hospice in small ways, we gird ourselves for greater—and braver—participation in the future.

33. Claim your superpower.

From the time she was a young girl, Zora Colakovic aspired to be a superhero. Unlike most children, she didn't just nurture her dream by playing games or reading comic books; she went into training. At age twelve she made a list of all the skills she figured she'd need, and then she set out to master them one by one. She kept updating her list until she was in her twenties, checking off what she'd accomplished, deleting some things, and adding new ones. The list included: flying helicopters and planes, parachuting, riding camels and elephants, throwing knives, shooting guns, martial arts, bomb diffusion, evasive driving, wilderness survival, speaking Russian, scuba diving, herbology, tracking animals and humans, and shooting bazookas. Even metaphysics was on the list, since Zora reckoned that a superhero had to have a philosophy to support her physical prowess. After receiving her PhD in Geopolitics, she applied to the CIA, convinced that it was the perfect career for her, her true "home," the one absolutely right job where she could manifest her many skills and be of service to a world in need. When she was rejected, she fell into a depression that lasted months.[1]

Zora's vision is compelling, her drive inspiring. The radio show *This American Life* did a story about her, and for a while Brad Pitt and Jennifer Anniston considered making a movie. It is compelling to think that we can systematically and with great discipline work our way out of our lowly human condition and maybe even save the world. What is your version of a superpower? Do you dream of having one of those Marvel Comics superpowers, like invisibility, telekinesis, or time travel? Or is it something that, though it may be physically possible, is nonetheless daunting for an ordinary human to attain, like beating the world record for running a marathon or curing a dread disease? Do you dream of buffing up into a bodybuilder who can lift hundreds of pounds? Do you want to be a fashion supermodel whose face appears on all the top magazines?

Or perhaps your aim arises from a lack in your own life, and you are determined to give your children the kind of upbringing you never received?

As for me, I wanted to write obsessively. For years my role model was the French novelist, cultural commentator, and celebrity gadabout André Malraux. I distinctly remember the impact of reading his obituary on the front page of the *New York Times* one night in 1976, when I was taking the crosstown bus from the west to the east side of Manhattan after having dinner with a friend. The article reported that, even in the last weeks of his life, Malraux had written twenty hours a day. Such discipline, I thought admiringly, such commitment to the task. I was in my twenties, trying to make my way in New York, longing to get a book of poetry published and chafing against the imaginary obstacles that held me back, while denying the real ones, like my increasing dependence on alcohol and a suspicion, masked by bravado, of my own mediocrity. Malraux's stern regime was a call to commitment. In a surge of willfulness I determined to be the kind of person who, if I couldn't actually write twenty hours a day, would at least shove everything else aside in an effort to do so. I never managed it. I never even came close. But Malraux's example did spur me on to keep trying, even when rejections and discouragement threatened to set me back.

Four decades later, I decided to read more about Malraux's compulsion. What had he been working on at the time, I wondered, that so drove him? Had he held himself to that punishing schedule before he got ill or had it been the advance of death that lashed him on? Google would reveal all. A brief search brought to my computer screen his front-page obituary. But there was absolutely no mention of Malraux writing twenty hours a day or, indeed, anything at all about his writing habits. Further delving into the internet yielded the information that the only relationship Malraux ever seemed to have had to such a feat of literary endurance was his own essay on T.E. Lawrence, "Demon of the Absolute," in which he describes Lawrence bent daily for that span of time over his *Seven Pillars of*

Wisdom. I had never read that essay. So how did I get the propulsive idea that Malraux had written twenty hours a day? His embodiment of that discipline had been a will o' the wisp, and yet it had been a superpower I had needed to believe in and aspire to.

Real superpowers are usually more subtle than we might imagine. Unlike the skill I'd attributed to Malraux, when I thought toughing it out was a mark of genius, the real superpowers we actually possess are personal qualities we often dismiss because they seem *too* natural. Zora Colakovic had a lot of skills, but she was overlooking her own superpower, which was probably something like a fierce ability to know the path she needed to take in her life and the determination to follow that path all the way to its conclusion. A young man I know used to ask all his friends what their superpowers were. Most people hemmed and hedged and came up with modest traits like, "I'm good with people" or "You can rely on me in an emergency." He kept prodding, urging them to be less humble. He wanted people to identify something other than a quality that another person might say in praise of them. He was encouraging them to name that innate and outstanding light that radiated from them, something as much a part of their being as those traits with which cartoon superheroes are physically endowed after exposure to a toxic ore or the bite of a spider. Self-exaltation is hard for most people. They don't want to boast, even to themselves. My friend, this young elicitor of superpowers, gently kept at it, coaxing people and querying until they came up with things like, "I am enchanted and I enchant other people" or "I bring people together who need to know each other but haven't met yet." The video team Soul Pancake posed the superpower question to people ranging in age from infancy to 100. The answers were delightful: "I'm really good at making a trumpet noise with my mouth" (20-year-old woman). "I go out and walk every single morning for two miles" (95-year-old man). "I have two superpowers. I can make anybody smile. And I can fart on command" (55-year-old woman)! "I can camouflage, because I got camouflage pants and camouflage shoes from

175

Amazon" (5-year-old boy).

What is your superpower? Are you a great listener? Are you the most loyal friend anybody's ever had? Do you know how to play with the world? Are you unafraid of the wounds of others? That's the superpower of Joanna Burgess, a nurse who specializes in wound care, a field she chose because of her own experience. For decades she had been ashamed of the urostomy, or bladder bag, she'd worn since she was a three-year-old child who survived a rare form of cancer. So weakened were her bones and organs from the radiation treatments she'd received that had saved her life that, as an adult, she also had to undergo a colostomy, a procedure to remove part of the colon and bring what remains out of the lining of the stomach to be fitted with a bag that collects waste. What changed for Joanna was that she stopped hiding her story and started telling it. First she told it to other adults at a retreat for people with life-altering illnesses. Then she told her patients who had had ostomies, then the other nurses whose duty was to care for those patients and help them over a bodily transition they often found humiliating. In 2011 Joanna received the Great Comebacks Award, a national program that recognizes individuals who have overcome bowel or bladder disease resulting in ostomy surgery and have been inspirational both in their personal lives and in what they have given to their communities. By now she has told her story at many conferences and media outlets. She told one interviewer, "My experience is that people either run far away from a very traumatic experience or they run toward it. I've always run toward it. When I go in and face someone who's new to ostomy surgery, they're in shock. My goal is not only to help them learn how to live again, but to live well. I often tell people that it's possible to find joy in sorrow and grace in scars. When a cancer patient says to me, 'I wouldn't take back my cancer, because it made me the person I wanted to be,' to me that is radical joy."

What is your superpower? Deep down you know what it is. Take some time to tease it out and identify it. And don't be shy! Be clear and proud about it. Where would Wonder Woman be if she simply said, "I'm pretty good in an emergency"? When you identify your superpower, tweak it and magnify it, so it sounds brilliant and heroic. So it sounds like something that was bestowed upon you under extraordinary circumstances. Then write it down and stick the piece of paper somewhere so you notice it often. It's important to know your superpower, because you're going to need it. In the midst of crises, it's easy to lose our tempers, lose our will, or lose our ability to cope. Throughout a pandemic and the trials of climate change, as well as in the personal tragedies that befall every one of us, our world, whether that constitutes our immediate family or a whole nation, will need us to be braver, more creative, more compassionate and, yes, more joyful than we feel easily able to be. When bad things happen to good people, good people get angry, confused, demanding, and scared, and they need allies who can grasp the complexities of the situation and bring calmness, compassion, and attention where it's called for. Manifesting our superpowers in those circumstances will be vital. Meanwhile we can exercise them in our regular lives, so as to keep them toned, like muscles. We need to acknowledge them and build them up instead of modestly depreciating them. We need to seek out occasions to put them to work.

What is your superpower? Even if you've never revealed it to anyone else, chances are those who know you would nod knowingly if you whispered it in their ear.

34. Do it though no one notices.

Do I really have to shred all this stuff? I asked myself as I considered the papers I'd found after I pried open the drawer of an old file cabinet in the attic. The contents had turned out to be ten years of Andy's tax returns, from when he was married to his first wife. Both were artists and teachers, and the stack on the floor was thick. Shredding all that paper would take hours. However, it didn't seem like a good idea to relegate sensitive information such as social security numbers and pension accounts to the recycling center. Just this once, I thought, just this once, I'll dump it all in a garbage bag and put it out on the road for trash pickup. I consider myself a conscientious environmentalist, but (the rationalization kicked in) it's only been four months since Andy died, and I'm dealing with a lot right now. And anyhow, who would know?

Every circumstance, every slight shift in the wind of my reality, forces me to make a decision. How I decide defines my existence. We are free, as Sartre insisted, to decide anything except not decide. An essential tool for surviving sorrow and living with meaning is to do the thing that must be done, simply because we know it must be done—whether anyone else cares or not, notices or not. It can be challenging to live by the standards and values we proclaim, the ones we endeavor to live by and wish others would live by too, and that's especially true when we're under duress. Sometimes it just seems reasonable to take the easier route. Claiming your superpower is about how you act in the world *for* the world. Doing what you know you must do is about manifesting your superpower in private as well. It's being your own hero at those times when nobody else seems to be paying the slightest attention.

Who doesn't love a story about striving resolutely and finally succeeding? Jack Andraka was fifteen years old when he came up with an idea for a more efficient test for pancreatic cancer. He wrote up a proposal, along with a request to conduct research in a medical lab and started sending it out. One hundred ninety-nine labs rejected him before Johns Hopkins School of Medicine finally realized the possibilities and accepted him. The diagnostic test Andraka developed turned out to be twenty-eight times faster, twenty-six thousand times less expensive, and more than one hundred times more sensitive than any of those currently in use. J.K. Rowling was unemployed, newly divorced, and trying to manage on welfare when she wrote her first book about a boy who studies magic. Twelve publishers turned it down before one of them signed her on. Harry Potter is now a figure recognized worldwide, and Rowling's estimated net worth is $650 million. Oprah Winfrey was fired from her first job as a TV anchor, because her bosses thought her tendency to get emotionally involved with the people she was interviewing damaged her credibility as a reporter. It is her way of being authentically interested in and compassionate toward her guests that has made her not only famous, but famously loved. The message behind these stories is clear: keep pushing and eventually you'll succeed.

Eventually also, truth be told, you might *not* succeed. The question is, will you keep blazing your particular trail anyway? The commitment to blazing with no guarantee of success might seem at first like capitulating to disbelief, proceeding as if the blatant reality confronting you—rejection after rejection—does not exist. Both reflect a will to bypass the roadblocks and forge ahead in circumstances that may be beyond your control. In fact, they are very different. Disbelief would have you ignore your reality. Doing what you must do accepts reality fully and then keeps going, despite the discouragement and outrage and, just possibly, the self-pity that goes along with it.

Stories about someone's commitment to doing what they must do, even if nobody else seems to notice or care, typically spotlight people like those in the examples above, famous people who've persevered and then achieved big. Far more often, taking the action that aligns with our personal ideals entails nothing so grand. It's the small things, the daily details that demand our resolve. It's living by the standards we espouse. I know a woman in Portland, Oregon who has determined that she will only buy from thrift stores. She calls herself a "radical conservative." She isn't writing a book or even a blog about her noble deed; she's just doing it because she is deeply bothered by rampant consumerism and the easy access the internet provides to enticing new products that require the labor of people who are poorly paid and the release of tons of carbon dioxide to get them to a door in America. I also know a young woman in North Carolina who takes her beer bottles home after she goes out to the local bar with friends, because she wants to make sure they are properly recycled. There are many stories in this book of people who take beautiful actions simply because they are compelled to do so, from sixteen-year-old Safie and her friends who bury dead animals to the families who brought Christmas lights and cheer to their burned neighborhood.

According to the second century AD Roman writer Apuleius, every one of us is accompanied through life by our own daemon, a semi-divine figure whose mission is to direct us along the paths that will help us fulfill our highest purpose in life, while steering us away from situations and behaviors that aren't good for us. With convincing authority Apuleius described the characteristics of this guiding, guarding being. Daemons have bodies "less dense and more attenuated than clouds." They "consist of that most pure, liquid, and serene element of air, and on this account are not easily visible to the human eye, unless they exhibit an image of themselves by divine command." Anyone who is wise enough not to ignore the counsel of their daemon is bound to be rewarded, whereas those who ignore the advice is likely to stumble. A daemon, says Apuleius, will gladly assume a variety of roles on the human's behalf, becoming:

> the one who can see to the bottom of uncertain situations and can give warning in desperate situations, can protect us in dangerous situations, and can come to our rescue when

we are in need, [intervene] now through a dream and now through a sign, or he can even step in by appearing personally in order to fend off evil, to reinforce the good, to lift up the soul in defeat, to steady our inconstancy, to lighten our darkness, to direct what is favorable toward us and to compensate what is evil.[1]

I aspire to heed my daemon, the authoritative, credible, and trustworthy aspect of myself that directs me in all I do. I want to do the things I'm called to do, whether they are convenient or potentially rewarding or not. I want to take the steps that I, and I alone, am directed to do at any particular moment. Even if no one else is watching, my daemon is.

In his farewell column to readers, journalist Nicholas Kristoff wrote that, although he had seen and chronicled a great deal of suffering and depravity during his thirty-seven-year career as a reporter for the *New York Times*, he had come to believe that "[t]alent is universal, even if opportunity is not." As an example he mentions the rickshaw drivers who pedaled through the gunfire during the Chinese massacre of protesters at Tiananmen Square in 1989, so that they could pick up the bodies of young people and carry them away from the carnage. They did this not to be noticed or thanked, but because it was a thing that needed doing. The greatest pool of gifted people in the world, Kristoff believed, are those who, despite lacking education and nurturing, have much to give.[2]

(Note: I ended up pulling the tax returns out of the garbage and shredding them, then taking the confettied paper to the recycling center.)

35. Imagine Sisyphus happy.

Sisyphus is condemned throughout eternity to push a boulder to the top of a mountain, only to watch it tumble back down to the bottom, where he must follow and retrieve it and make the journey again. And again and again and again. According to Camus, however, in his essay, "The Myth of Sisyphus," Sisyphus is not to be pitied. Far from it. The essay, remarkably, ends: "The struggle itself toward the heights is enough to fill [one's] heart. One must imagine Sisyphus happy." How could such a nightmare bring anything like happiness to Sisyphus? Although Camus reflects that the condemned man did get a welcome break every time he made his way back down the mountain to rejoin his rock for the next slogging ascent, that's not the reason he might be considered anything but despondent. No, says Camus, his happiness rests in his commitment to doing this difficult, impossible thing with acute awareness of the necessity of doing it. All his energy is present. His muscles are aligned to the task. He undertakes his task as if each time he begins to heave that rock to the top of the mountain is the first time and also the last time.

Imagine now that you are Sisyphus on the peak. You've succeeded—at least for now! You've managed to shove your rock to the top once more, and you can take a breath of self-congratulatory relief. You experience a surge of gratitude for the ground itself that has supported you all the way along your arduous journey. A breeze riffles the trees, and the leaves clap for your success. Unfortunately, this jubilant moment bestows no promise that you're absolved from the next round of pushing. It's likely that you'll still have to trudge back down the mountain and get behind your boulder again. Now you know, however, that there is a way through and that how you make the journey counts for everything. There will be tiny oases along the way. You will find friendship and understanding among others. Magical things will happen at the most unlikely of times. You will experience outrageous happiness. Accepting the reality of hard times is actually liberating, because it shoves you down to the hard place where you're forced to decide, *Will I capitulate to despair and helplessness or will I survive as magnificently as possible through it all?*

Faced with climate change, the death of the ones we love most in the world, the loss of the places that are dear to our hearts and the animals and plants that used to thrive among us, faced with the likelihood of yet more pandemics, political unrest, and racial intolerance, I need to be Sisyphus. You need to be Sisyphus. We all need to be Sisyphus. We cannot confront any emergency, whether it is personal, local, or global, by hoping and praying that the problem will go away or waiting for somebody else to act. We cannot avoid hardship and the grief and worry that accompany it. Probably, we will never be fully prepared when it crashes into us, and we will be knocked off our feet.

We can, however, determine how we'll respond to our challenges, whatever they may be. Because how we respond will save our life. If we do not deny our heartbreak, if we give it full expression, it will not toxify inside us like a hard lump of poison that becomes ever more lethal the longer it remains untreated. By expressing our grief through tears, creative work, and sharing our lives and our stories with others, both known and unknown, we soften that grief and discover compassion and gratitude infiltrating it. By opening up to the possibility of wonder from surprising sources, we recognize that, even in the bleakest of times, beauty is possible and aimed right at us. By absorbing that beauty whenever it strikes, we gain a wider perspective of our own situation and the world at large, all of us citizens of Earth burdened, suffering, crazy, delightful and delighted, laughing, striving, loving, and stumbling all over the place. We become a part of the whole, and we see ourselves as whole. By giving back beauty whenever the opportunity arises, we transform our surroundings and our own perspective. In the hardest of times, we know ourselves to be not only survivors but wild, indefatigable forces who never cease to create a new reality, not by ignoring the old and troubling one, but by grabbing hold of it and using its very materials to shape something new. We weave beauty out of scraps of debris. Even as we are being flattened, made nearly breathless with sorrow and worry, some life force within us shouts, "I want to live! I *will* live!"

No matter what we go through, no matter how old we get, we know that there is no end of our push to the heights. We accept our task and do so with gratitude, for we know that our sorrow and despair are only our surroundings. Like Peter V., who punched through the avalanche, as long as we can lift an arm and push forward, do just the smallest thing, take just the feeblest action to reach beyond our own confinement into the greater world, then we are not powerless. Joyfully we take on our endless task, even if no one thanks us, even if no one notices, even if, to all appearances, it makes no measurable difference whatsoever to anyone else. We do it because we must, because our life depends on it, because, we know with all our heart that being the alive human that we are means doing what we are compelled to do, opening ourselves up to the world. This is how we live with sorrow and, extraordinarily, in the midst of it experience immense joy.

NOTES

1. Refuse to disbelieve.

[1] Albert Camus, *The Plague*, trans. Stuart Gilbert (New York: Vintage Books, 1972), 36.

[2] Bill McKibben, *Falter: Has the Human Game Begun to Play Itself Out?*, (New York: Holt Paperbacks, 2019), 121.

[3] Timothy Morton, *Hyperobjects: Philosophy and Ecology after the End of the World* (Minneapolis: University of Minnesota Press, 2013), 1.

[4] Hannah Arendt, *Men in Dark Times* (New York: A Harvest Book / Harcourt Brace & Company, 1993), 23.

2. Drop into the well of grief.

[1] Ken Burns, *Jazz*, PBS Miniseries, 2001, Episode 1.

[2] Francis Weller, *The Wild Edge of Sorrow* (Berkeley: North Atlantic Books, 2015), 9.

[3] Marcel Merleau-Ponty, *Phenomonology of Perception*, trans. Colin Smith (New York: Routledge & Kegan Paul, 1962), 83.

4. Evolve mourning.

[1] Glenn Albrecht, *Earth Emotions: New Words for a New World* (Ithaca: Cornell University Press, 2019), 78, 79, 86.

[2] W.S. Merwin, *The Mays of Ventadorn* (Washington, DC: National Geographic, 2002), 46-47.

[3] Quoted in Carl Safina, *Beyond Words: What Animals Think and Feel* (New York: Henry Holt and Company, 2015), ix.

[4] Ibid, 360.

⁵ Richard Grant, "Do Trees Talk to Each Other?", Smithsonian Magazine online, March 2018. https://www.smithsonianmag.com/science-nature/the-whispering-trees-180968084/

⁶ Rick Steves, *Rich Steves Europe*, Program 620, "Frankfurt; Ghostways; Where I Really Want to Go," Nov. 21, 2021.

⁷ Martín Prechtel, *The Smell of Rain on Dust* (Berkeley: North Atlantic Books, 2015), 36-37.

⁸ Melissa Holbrook Pierson, *The Place You Love Is Gone: Progress Hits Home* (New York: W.W. Norton & Co., 2006), 58.

⁹ Sarah Anne Edwards and Linda Buzzell, "The Waking-Up Syndrome," in *Ecotherapy: Healing with Nature in Mind,* eds. Linda Buzzell and Craig Chalquist (San Francisco: Sierra Club Books, 2009), 127.

5. Resist the temptation to suffer alone.

¹ Joanna Macy in *Climate Crisis as a Spiritual Path*, Anne Macksound and John Ankele, Old Dog Documentaries, 2013, with a 20-minute excerpt edited in 2021, https://vimeo.com/588455489.

² Edward O. Wilson and David Sloan Wilson, "Evolution 'for the Good of the Group,' " *American Scientist*, September-October, 2008, https://www.americanscientist.org/article/evolution-for-the-good-of-the-group.

³ Robert Jay Lifton, *Death In Life: Survivors of Hiroshima* (New York: Random House, 1967), 176-77.

⁴ Zoom, a small company that offered a free version of its product and made it easier for students, colleagues at work, and friends to connect, saw profit rise 136 times between February and April, 2020, from $198,000 for the same period in 2019 to $27 million in 2020. "Zoom booms as teleconferencing company profits from coronavirus crisis," Associated Press, June 2, 2020, https://www.theguardian.com/technology/2020/jun/03/zoom-booms-as-teleconferencing-company-profits-from-coronavirus-crisis.

6. Abandon hope.

[1] Barbara Ehrenreich, "Welcome to Cancerland," *Harper's*, November 2001, 47-53.

7. Punch through the avalanche.

[1] Melanie J. Randle and Richard Eckersley, "Public perceptions of future threats to humanity and different societal responses: a cross-national study," University of Wollongong, Faculty of Business, 2015, https://ro.uow.edu.au/cgi/viewcontent.cgi?article=1742&context=buspapers

[2] Wallace Stevens, "The Well Dressed Man with a Beard," in *The Palm at the End of the Mind: Selected Poems and a Play*, ed. Holly Stevens (New York: Vintage Books, 1972), 190.

[3] K.M. McIntyre, E. Puterman, J.M. Scodes, T.-H., Choo, C.J. Choi, M. Pavlicova, & R.P. Sloan, "The effects of aerobic training on subclinical negative affect: A randomized controlled trial. *Health Psychology, 39*(4), 255–264, https://psycnet.apa.org/record/2020-00792-001

[4] "Greta Thunberg's Father: 'She is happy, but I worry,'" BBC News, December 30, 2019, https://www.bbc.com/news/uk-50901789.

8. Dare.

[1] David Schoen, "Katrina's Happy Victim," *The Oakland Tribune*, March 12, 2006, http://www.freerepublic.com/focus/f-news/1593405/posts.

[2] Courtney Miles ended up moving to Oakland, California to live with an uncle he had never met/ He enrolled in high school, where he joined the basketball team and did well in his academic work.

[3] Lewis Gordon, "Living Thought, Living Freedom: A Lecture in Black Existential Philosophy," Southern Illinois University Edwardsville, March 4, 2014, YouTube, https://www.bing.com/videos/search?q=Black+existentialism&view=detail&mid=2CFEEF83FD980A58E6942CFEEF83FD980A58E694&FORM=VIRE.

[4] Peter Trachtenberg, *The Book of Calamities* (New York: Little Brown & Company, 2008), 387.

9. Do it because only you can.

[1] Rachel Denhollander, *What Is a Girl Worth: My Story of Breaking the Silence and Exposing the Truth About Larry Nassar and USA Gymnastics* (New York: Tyndedale House Publishers, 2019), xii.

[2] Sarah Anne Edwards and Linda Buzzell, "The Waking-Up Syndrome," in *Ecotherapy: Healing with Nature in Mind*, ed. Linda Buzzell and Craig Chalquist (San Francisco: Sierra Club Books, 2009), 129-30.

10. Release the old reality.

[1] "Your stories: Through the eyes of a COVID nurse who tested positive," *HIMSS News*, April 24, 2020, https://www.healthcareitnews.com/news/your-stories-through-eyes-covid-nurse-who-tested-positive.

11. Sing through the darkest night.

[1] "52 Steps to Heaven," *South African History Online*, January 16, 2012, https://www.sahistory.org.za/archive/52-steps-heaven. See also: Black Sash, 1989, 42, https://www.csvr.org.za/publications/1381-life-after-death-row-post-traumatic-stress-and-the-story-of-philip-takedi. "The first thing you notice as you come into Central is the singing, the sound of the Condemneds. Up behind the huge sign in the hall saying Stilte/Silence, the Condemneds sing, chant, sing through the day and before an execution, through the night. At times the chant is quiet, a distant murmur of quiet humming softly. Then it swells: you can hear a more strident urgent note in the swell, sounding through the prison, singing the hymns that will take them through the double doors into the gallows. Condemneds, waiting their turn, singing their fellows through their last nights."

[2] "The Italians Making Music on Balconies Under Coronavirus Quarantine." the *New Yorker* (online), March 20, 2020, https://www.youtube.com/watch?v=EBByYjjvNzs.

[3] Ehrenreich, *Dancing in the Streets: A History of Collective Joy* (New York: Henry Holt and Company, 2006), 261.

12. Fight the angel—and let her win.

[1] Rainer Maria Rilke, "The Man Watching," *Selected Poems of Rainer Maria Rilke*, trans. Robert Bly (New York: Harper & Row, 1981), 106.

13. Open up to the possibility of mystery.

[1] Jose Ortega y Gasset, *Meditations on Hunting,* trans. Howard Wescott (New York: Charles Scribner's Sons, 1972), 150.

[2] Carl Safina, *Becoming Wild* (New York: Henry Holt, 2020), 12.

14. Look for where the smiling ends.

[1] Rainer Maria Rilke, from *The Notes of Malte Laurid Brigge,* in Walter Kaufmann, ed., *Existentialism from Dostoevsky to Sartre* (New York: Meridien, 1975), 141.

15. Bear responsibility. Don't collapse under it.

[1] Union of Concerned Scientists, "Ten Signs of Global Warming," *Reports & Multimedia/Explainer,* April 4, 2017 (Updated December 7, 2017), https://www.ucsusa.org/resources/ten-signs-global-warming.

[2] Elizabeth Marks, Caroline Hickman, Panu Pihkala, Susan Clayton, Eric R. Lewandowski, Elouise E. Mayall, Britt Wray, Catriona Mellor, and Lise van Susteren, "Young People's Voices on Climate Anxiety, Government Betrayal and Moral Injury: A Global Phenomenon," Published in *The Lancet,* September 7, 2021, SSRN: https://ssrn.com/abstract=3918955.

[3] William R. Jordan III, *The Sunflower Forest: Ecological Restoration and the New Communion with Nature* (Berkeley, CA: University of California Press, 2003), 46. Jordan, citing religious scholar Jonathan Z. Smith, posits that shame arose when agriculturalists began to kill for food the animals they had raised.

[4] Jon Wallace, "Pride tops guilt as a motivator for environmental decisions," High Meadows Environmental Institute (Princeton: Princeton University, February 14, 2018), https://environment.princeton.edu/news/pride-tops-guilt-as-a-motivator-for-environmental-decisions/.

16. Imagine the end of the world—but not the end of the story.

[1] Shierry Weber Nicholsen, *The Love of Nature and the End of the World: The Unspoken Dimensions of Environmental Concern* (Cambridge: MIT Press, 2003), 131.

[2] Ibid, 154.

[3] Jason Zinoman, "An Age-Old Bite of the Vampire Metaphor," the *New York Times*, October 31, 2021, Section ST, 10.

[4] Elissa Nadworny, "Why Teens Find The End Of The World So Appealing," December 18, 2017, 6:01 AM ET, *All Things Considered*, NPR.org, https://www.npr.org/sections/ed/2017/12/18/536007249/why-teens-find-the-end-of-the-world-so-appealing.

[5] Robert Jay Lifton, *The Climate Swerve: Reflections on Mind, Hope and Survival* (New York: The New Press, 2017), 154.

[6] Jim Collins, *Good to Great: Why Come Companies Make the Leap and Others Don't* (New York: HarperCollins, 2001), 84-85.

17. Explore what you think you already know.

[1] Stan Rushworth in *Living in the Time of Dying*, Director Michael Shaw, 2020, https://www.livinginthetimeofdying.com/documentary.

[2] Timothy Morton, *Being Ecological* (Cambridge: MIT Press, 2018), 76.

[3] Greg Allen, "Escaping New Orleans by Water," *Weekend Edition*, NPR, September 3, 2005.

18. Be on the lookout for your next teacher.

[1] "Voiceless Blowing Sound," Interview with Vi Hilbert, interviewed by Laura Simms, *Parabola*, Vol. 25, No. 3, Fall 2000, 65.

20. Redefine nature.

[1] J. Phoenix Smith, "Children and Nature: Remembering Trayvon Martin," Blog, *Ecosoulwisdom*, February 28, 2013, http://www.ecosoulwisdom.org/children-and-nature-remembering-trayvon-martin-2/.

[2] William Cronon, "Introduction," in *Uncommon Ground: Rethinking the Human Place in Nature* (New York: W.W. Norton & Company, 1996), 35.

[3] Since a river cannot speak for itself, who will determine how it exercises these rights? This article points out that in New Zealand the rights of the river will be determined by the indigenous Iwi people, whereas in India, it will be government that makes decisions for the Ganges and Yamuna. Mari Margil, Ashish Kothari and Shrishtee Bajpai, "Now rivers have the same legal status as people, we must uphold their rights," *The Guardian* on line, April 21, 2017, https://www.theguardian.com/global-development-professionals-network/2017/apr/21/rivers-legal-human-rights-ganges-whanganui.

[4] Andrew Blackwell, *Visit Sunny Chernobyl And Other Adventures in the World's Most Polluted Places* (New York: Rodale, 2012), 268.

21. Let beauty seduce you.

[1] Morton, *Being Ecological*, 124-25.

[2] Viktor Frankl, *Man's Search for Meaning* (New York: Pocket Books, 1984), 59.

22. Transcend downward.

[1] Mircea Eliade, *Myths, Dreams, and Mysteries: The Encounter between Contemporary Faiths and Archaic Realities*, trans. Philip Mairet (New York: Harper Colophon, 1960), 106.

[2] Loren Eiseley, "The Bird and the Machine," in *The Star Thrower* (New York: A Harvest (HBJ) Book, 1978), 88.

[3] Neil Evernden interview in Derrick Jensen, *Listening to the Land: Conversations about Nature, Culture, and Eros* (San Francisco: Sierra Club, 1995), 119.

[4] Wendell Berry, *Leavings: Poems* (Berkeley: Counterpoint, 2010), 92.

23. Open up to the marvel of others.

[1] Andre Breton, *Nadja*, trans. Richard Howard (New York: Grove Press, 1960), 71.

24. Play.

[1] Kate Cray, "How the Coronavirus Is Influencing Children's Play," *The Atlantic*, April 1, 2020, https://www.theatlantic.com/family/archive/2020/04/coronavirus-tag-and-other-games-kids-play-during-a-pandemic/609253/.

[2] Robert J. Landy, "Drama Therapy with Adults," in *Play Therapy with Adults*, ed. Charles E. Schaefer (Hoboken, NJ: John Wiley & Songs, Inc., 2003), 31.

25. Inquire into the mystery of objects coming alive.

[1] Kris Pannecoucke, "They call us bewitched': the DRC performers turning trash into art," Photo essay, *The Guardian*, August 20, 2021, https://www.theguardian.com/global-development/2021/aug/20/they-call-us-bewitched-the-drc-performers-turning-trash-into-art-photo-essay?utm_term=675d83d7c9c787a49d14e8cd7afde533&utm_campaign=GlobalDispatch&utm_source=esp&utm_medium=Email&CMP=globaldispatch_email.

[2] Graham Harman, "On the Undermining of Objects," in *The Speculative Turn: Continental Materialism and Realism*, ed. Levi Brant, Nich Srnicek, and Graham Harman (Melbourne: re.press series, 2011), 25-26.

[3] JoAnna Klein, "Taking the Pulse of a Sandstone Tower in Utah," the *New York Times* online, September 9, 2019, https://www.nytimes.com/2019/09/09/science/castleton-tower-utah-vibration.html.

26. Bear witness.

[1] Wislawa Szymborska, "Hunger Camp at Jaslo," trans. Grazyna Drabik and Austin Flint, in *Against Forgetting: Twentieth Century Poetry of Witness*, ed. Carolyn Forché (New York: W.W. Norton & Company, 1995), 460.

[2] Susan Sontag, *Regarding the Pain of Others* (New York: Picador, 2003), 42.

[3] Thomas Dooling, "And Nothing But the Truth," in *Parabola*, Vol. 11, No. 1, Spring 1986, 65.

4 Abraham Verghese, MD, "Close Encounter of the Human Kind," *New York Times Magazine*. Sept. 18, 2005, 192.

5 Trachtenberg, *Book of Calamities*, 397)

6 Bernie Glassman, *Bearing Witness: A Zen Master's Lessons in Making Peace* (New York: Bell Tower, 1998), 110.

7 Pema Chödrön, *When Things Fall Apart: Heart Advice for Difficult Times* (Boston: Shambhala, 2000), 93.

27. Go home.

1 Lewis Gordon, "Living Thought, Living Freedom," https://www.bing.com/videos/search?q=Black+existentialism&view=detail&mid=2CFEEF83FD980A58E6942CFEEF83FD980A58E694&FORM=VIRE
2 Mark Epstein, *Advice Not Given: A Guide to Getting Over Yourself* (New York: Penguin Books, 2018), 20.

Give

1 Marcel Mauss, *The Gift: Forms and Functions of Exchange in Archaic Societies* (New York: W.W. Norton & Company, 1967), 69.

28. Say goodbye to a glacier.

1 Lacy M. Johnson, "How to Mourn a Glacier, the *New Yorker*, October 20, 2019, https://www.newyorker.com/news/dispatch/how-to-mourn-a-glacier.

2 Friedrich Nietzsche, from *The Gay Science*, in Walter Kaufmann, *Existentialism...*, 126.

3 Tony Hiss, *The Experience of Place*, (New York: Alfred A. Knopf, 1990), xii.

29. Make beauty behavioral.

1 Paul Bloom, "The Moral Life of Babies," the *New York Times*, May 5, 2010, https://www.nytimes.com/2010/05/09/magazine/09babies-t.html.

[2] Joshua Gordon, "The Kindness of Strangers: Supporting Each Other During COVID-19," Director's Message, NIH (National Institute of Mental Health), May 7, 2020, https://www.nimh.nih.gov/about/director/messages/2020/the-kindness-of-strangers-supporting-each-other-during-covid-19.shtml.

[3] Jean Case, "Five Signs For Hope after Harvey and Irma," *Forbes*, September 12, 2017, 5:29 PM, https://www.forbes.com/sites/jeancase/2017/09/12/five-signs-for-hope-after-harvey-and-irma/#5ec068aa1215.

[4] Colleen Walsh, "Money spent on others can buy happiness," Harvard News Office, the *Harvard Gazette*, April 17, 2008, https://greatergood.berkeley.edu/article/item/5_ways_giving_is_good_for_you.

[5] Jamil Zaki, "Kindness Contagion" Witnessing kindness inspires kindness, causing it to spread like a virus," *Scientific American*, July 26, 2016, https://www.scientificamerican.com/article/kindness-contagion/.

[6] Anna Primavesi, "The Preoriginal Gift—and Our Response to It," in *Ecospirit: Religions and Philosophies for the Earth*, eds. Laurel Kearns and Catherine Keller (New York: Fordham University Press, 2007), 230.

[7] David Treuer, "The Ceremony," the *New York Times Magazine*, September 5, 2021, 31.

30. Donate patience.

[1] Jennifer Sweeton,"How to Heal the Traumatized Brain," *Psychology Today*, March 13, 2017, https://www.psychologytoday.com/us/blog/workings-well-being/201703/how-heal-the-traumatized-brain.

[2] *1A*, Laura Bliss, reporter with Bloomberg City Lab, WSKG radio, November 18, 2021.

[3] Robbyn McFadden, producer, and Carol A. Ross, editor, "Impatience: Why we don't want to wait, and what we can do about it," *CBS News Sunday Morning*, October 25, 2020, https://www.cbsnews.com/news/impatience-why-we-dont-want-to-wait-what-we-can-do-about-it/.

31. Get dirty.

[1] Glassman, *Bearing Witness*, 125.

32. Volunteer for Earth Hospice.

[1] Sarah Goodman, "Tests Find More Than 200 Chemicals in Newborn Umbilical Cord Blood," *Scientific American*, December 2, 2009, https://www.scientificamerican.com/article/newborn-babies-chemicals-exposure-bpa/.

[2] Allen Kim, "Climate change may doom 1 in 3 species of plants and animals in the next 50 years," CNN, February 21, 2020, https://www.cnn.com/2020/02/21/weather/species-extinction-climate-trnd/index.html

[3] Stephen and Ondrea Levine, *Who Dies: An Investigation of Conscious Living and Conscious Dying* (New York: Anchor Books, 1989), 200.

[4] Jared Diamond, *Collapse: How Societies Choose to Fail or Succeed* (New York: Penguin Books, 2006), 114.

[5] Jennifer L. Adams, "Environmental Hospice and Memorial as Redemption: Public Rituals for Renewal," *Western Journal of Communication*, April 16, 2020, https://doi.org/10.1080/10570314.2020.1753234.

33. Claim your superpower.

[1] "Wonder Woman," *This American Life*, produced by Kelly McEvers, February 23, 2001, https://www.thisamericanlife.org/archive?contributor=8887.

34. Do it though no one notices.

[1] Marie-Louise von Franz, "Daimons and the Inner Companion," *Parabola*, Vol. VI, No. 4, October 1991, pp. 41-42. Von Franz notes that, in its original form in Egypt and pre-Hellenic Greece, the *daimon* was "a momentarily perceptible divine activity, such as a startled horse, a failure in work, illnesses, madness, terror in certain natural spots."

[2] Nicholas Kristoff, "A Farewell to Readers, With Hope," the *New York Times*, October 21, 2021, SR3.

About the Author

Trebbe Johnson is the author of four previous books, including *Radical Joy for Hard Times: Finding Meaning and Making Beauty in Earth's Broken Places*, as well as many articles and essays that explore the human bond with nature and myth. She is the founder and director of the global community Radical Joy for Hard Times, devoted to finding and making beauty in hurt places. Trebbe speaks four languages; has camped alone in the Arctic wilderness; studied classical Indian dance; and worked as an artist's model, a street sweeper in an English village, and an award-winning multimedia producer. She has led contemplative journeys in a clear-cut forest, Ground Zero in New York, the Sahara Desert, and other places. She lives in Ithaca, New York.

Made in the USA
Middletown, DE
11 March 2023

26608953R00119